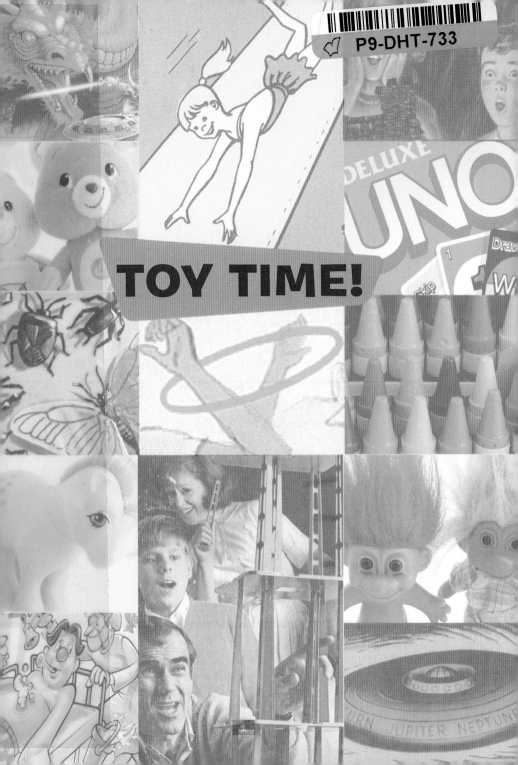

P9-DHT-733

DELUXE UNO

TOY TIME!

IT'S ALMOST ALIVE!

WIFFLE BALL®

Regulation
BASEBALL SIZE

A LOOK BACK at the MOST-BELOVED TOYS of DECADES PAST

OOMERANG
IT SAILS
IT FLIES

TOY TIME!

From
HULA HOOPS
to **HE-MAN**
to **HUNGRY HUNGRY HIPPOS**

Christopher Byrne

THREE RIVERS PRESS
NEW YORK

MAR 2014

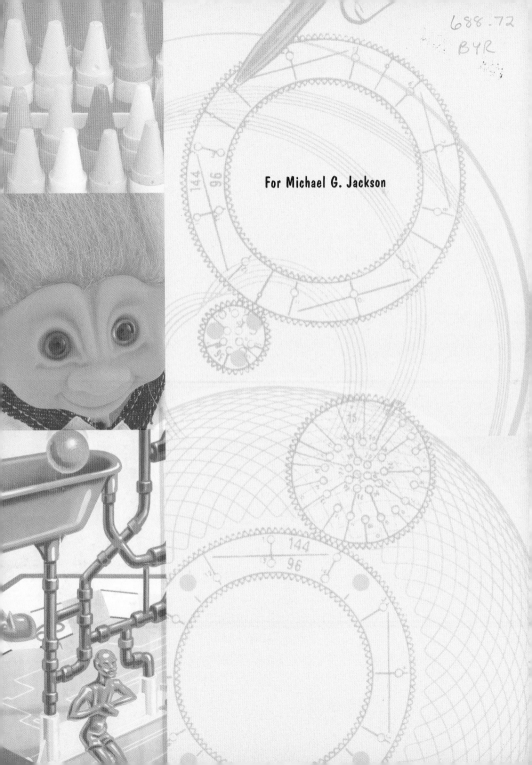

For Michael G. Jackson

contents

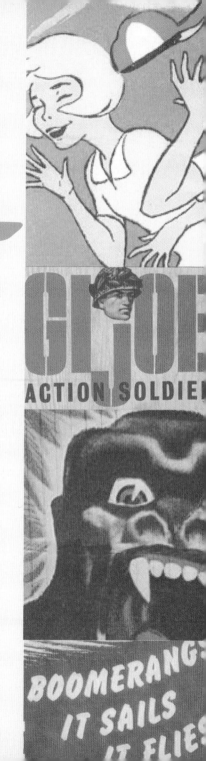

When I was growing up, I had the coolest toys!" How many times did I hear those words after I told someone I was putting together this book? Then, without fail, they would proceed to tell me I simply *had* to include hula hoops or He-Man or Hungry Hungry Hippos . . . or whatever had been their favorite toy.

And this would happen pretty much across the board, whether I was talking to someone in their twenties, their forties, or their seventies. Sure, the toys they recalled might have differed, but the pure joy with which they recalled them was the same. Over the past decade, as the Toy Guy and content director for TimetoPlayMag.com, I've spoken with hundreds of people about the toys they loved as children. What I've found again and again is that nothing makes a face light up quite like the memory of a favorite toy. Because it's through these playthings—some now old and battered and shoved in closets, others preserved in museums, and yet others commanding astronomical prices from collectors—that we summon up our most cherished memories. Toys have a totemic power on people, and revisiting and reflecting on them consistently touches the deep, emotional connection we have to our childhoods. They remind us of Christmases and birthdays, carefree summers, weekends spent idly playing, and all the other simple and innocent joys of being young. To look back at the toys we played with as children is to take a trip back in time.

So let me ask you this: What were *your* favorite toys? And how often have you found a common bond with other people of your generation—just based on the toys you played with as a child? Were you a Hot Wheels kid? A Matchbox man? Did you prefer My Little Pony to Care Bears? Idolize G.I. Joe or Major Matt Mason? No matter where and when they grew up, virtually everyone has some memory of a toy that starts a cascade of reminiscences and forges an immediate bond with others who shared those experiences. The toys we grew up with are part of our fabric, inextricably woven into both our memories and our collective identities as a generation.

But while the love of toys knows no boundaries, if you were a kid between the early 1960s and the '80s, you grew up during the golden age of toys. The post–World War II years saw an explosion of creativity that amused and delighted a generation of toy buyers.

As the culture shifted from agrarian to industrial to information based, children in the postwar era were afforded the luxury of being children longer and postponing adult responsibilities. Plus, after the war, plastics manufacturers were left with surplus material to put to peacetime uses, including the production of toys. Metal fabrication plants that had been cranking out munitions began to make swing sets, bicycles, scooters, and wagons. Thanks to wartime advances in manufacturing, toys were bigger, brighter, and more entertaining than ever. Better yet, the rising middle class now had the means to afford them.

And then there was television, of course. As the TV became a standard appliance in every home, the cultural experience was homogenized. Kids watched all the same shows—and all the same

commercials—and thus they clamored for all the same toys. This made it much easier for toy makers to hit on an idea, advertise the heck out of it, and sell as many as they could roll off the production lines.

But even as toys got fancier and flashier, it was never really so much about the toy as it was about the play. No matter how well the toys were designed, or how many fancy plastics or metals or computer chips they contained, the most beloved toys were always those that inspired an individual child's imagination. At the end of the day, the ability to spark the imagination will always be what sets apart the best toys—the ones that make the best memories.

This book is a celebration of toys and a window back on our memories. But given the hundreds of thousands of toys that have been produced over the years, how could anyone effectively curate a collection? After all, most everyone has a specific toy that tugs at their individual heartstrings, whether it was one they longed for and didn't get, or one they found wrapped and waiting for them on a holiday morning or on a birthday. So how did I go about selecting what I believe to be a shared pantheon of universally beloved toys?

Well, my team at TimetoPlayMag.com polled social media, reached out to our community, and simply *asked* people what toys they had loved most. This is in addition to the ongoing conversations my colleagues and I have all the time. Everyone loves to talk about their favorite toys. When it comes to play, it turns out, we're a lot more similar than we are divided. Much to my surprise, I found that across the generations, whether male or female and hailing from Connecticut to California and everywhere in between, we all cherish many of the same toys. Truly classic toys, I soon realized, are the threads that knit us all together: the shared cultural fabric that transcends everything—race, class, gender, and even time.

As I talked with people all over the United States, I heard stories that touched my heart and stories that made me howl with laughter. I couldn't find a single person who wasn't profoundly affected by the way they had played as a child. In this process, I confirmed something I've long known: All play is storytelling—whether through a doll, a car, a board game, or an action figure. And it is through these created stories that we let our imaginations run wild, explore our identities, and dream about our futures.

In short, this book is an exploration—and a celebration—of the almost magical effect toys have had on us individually and as a culture. In it, we'll look at the toys that were among the most beloved of the latter half of the twentieth century, and revisit just how those toys roused our imaginations, shaped our memories, and touched our lives.

So, read on and enjoy your journey back to a simpler, more innocent time—that is, Toy Time.

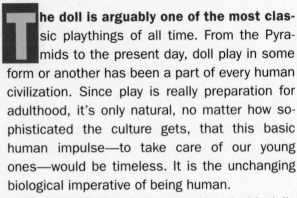

Chapter 1

My Dolly and Me

The doll is arguably one of the most classic playthings of all time. From the Pyramids to the present day, doll play in some form or another has been a part of every human civilization. Since play is really preparation for adulthood, it's only natural, no matter how sophisticated the culture gets, that this basic human impulse—to take care of our young ones—would be timeless. It is the unchanging biological imperative of being human.

But a big change in *how* we played with dolls would come in the middle of the twentieth century. While doll play had traditionally involved a little girl taking on the role of the mommy, as women's roles in the culture changed, so, too, did the roles of dolls. Baby dolls, of course, never went away (though they got new features and became more realistic as the decades went on); the fundamental instinct to nurture is something that seems to be wired into little girls no matter what else is going on.

In the post–World War II years, as the culture began to focus more on youth, and the teenager became something to be idolized (at least by little girls), dolls began to reflect different stages in girls' lives. They also began to be best friends, upending the traditional mother-daughter relationship between a little girl and her dolls. The most famous, of course, was Barbie, the Original Teenage Fashion Model, but she wasn't always the most popular. After all, what was a grown-up figure and a fancy wardrobe compared to a doll who could talk, like Chatty Cathy (introduced in 1959, the same year as Barbie), grow her hair, like Beautiful Crissy, and even drink, eat, and—yes—poop, like Baby Alive?

But whether best friend or baby, dolls have long been a way for little girls to begin the process of trying on roles and imagining their future lives.

Barbie 1959

No toy in history has been more exhaustively analyzed, written about, loved, and, frankly, loathed, than Barbie. Never before in the history of toys—or popular culture, for that matter—have a few ounces of plastic had such a profound impact on so many. Volumes have been written about her, and her importance as a cultural icon has been well known for more than half a century. To some she is an institution: a trendsetter that empowered and paved the way for millions of young women. To others, she is the emblem of what's wrong with our culture, promoting an unrealistic standard of beauty and forcing girls to adhere to dated and pernicious gender stereotypes.

WHY WE LOVED HER

Given her stature in the culture, Barbie's history has always been defined by this tension between the joy she has brought to millions and the controversy she has courted. But the fact of the matter is that Barbie, like any toy, "lives" only in the imagination. She is neither heroine nor villainess, but only what she is imagined to be. (A shrink would call that projection, and Barbie Millicent Rogers has had it all.) Fortunately, her little plastic shoulders have repeatedly proven more than equal to hold the weight placed on them over the years.

Barbie's history is well known, but it bears repeating that in the 1950s, when she first came on the scene, there was no such thing as a fashion doll. There were baby dolls, naturally, because girls were inevitably going to be mothers. But the only dolls that let girls play with fashion were paper dolls. As the story goes, the idea for Barbie was born when Ruth Handler, a partner in Mattel, watched her daughter, Barbara, and her friends playing with some paper dolls and found herself wishing there were a more lifelike fashion doll for girls, one that allowed them to act out being teenagers and even grown women. Despite what some of Barbie's detractors say about the doll today, Handler believed passionately that this type of play would help girls build their self-esteem.

So Handler approached the Mattel executives (all men), who rejected the idea. However, not long afterward, while on a trip to Germany, Ruth found a doll that appeared to validate her vision—and prove, at least to her, that a teenage doll would work with contemporary American kids. Called Lilli, the popular German doll confirmed Ruth's belief that there was a market for a doll that was grown-up and beautiful and had a killer wardrobe. She brought Lilli back to the United States and used it as a loose model to create an entirely new design for a slim, attractive eleven-and-a-half-inch-tall plastic doll. Ruth finally convinced Mattel to test the doll, and hired designer Charlotte Johnson to create the clothes. Finally, she named it Barbie in honor of her daughter.

At first, the toy trade was lukewarm on Barbie, the Original Teenage Fashion Model, in her black-and-white swimsuit and ponytail. They'd never seen anything like her, and they were dubious about her commercial prospects—that is, until little girls got her. First-year sales of the dolls topped three hundred thousand units at about four dollars each (a lot at the time), with fashions sold separately.

As the Barbie doll became a bigger and bigger hit, her world started to grow, as Skipper, Stacie, Kelly, Midge, Ken, and other friends joined her social circle.

WHY WE ALSO HATED HER

Still, it was not always smooth sailing for Barbie.

As the feminist movement emerged in the late 1960s and early '70s, as women were rejecting traditional roles, Barbie became anathema to the women's movement and almost became passé. That is, until Mattel's Jill Barad led a total revamping of the brand under the banner "We girls can do anything!"—somewhat mollifying many of Barbie's feminist detractors but more importantly lending her new relevance and appeal for a new generation of girls who came thronging to the restaged Barbie.

And then, there was the matter of Barbie's body. Long attacked for being an impossible representation of the human form (it is said that were she a real person, her narrow waist would be physically unable to support her ample bosom), Barbie's "real world" measurements (36–18–33) have always been a lightning rod for protests, thought to cause poor body image and lack of self-esteem in young, impressionable girls.

So in 1997, Mattel made a "more realistic" body for Barbie, and it bombed. It turned out that little girls didn't really care whether she looked like a real woman or not—they *liked* her familiar, rail-thin, fully developed body.

DID YOU KNOW?
The bestselling Barbie doll ever was the Totally Hair Barbie, with hair that reached to her toes, launched in 1992.

WHERE IS SHE NOW?

Barbie's "look," like that of any fashion icon, has been in a constant state of reinvention since she first came on the scene. For example, her pillbox hat of 1962 gave way to the Carnaby Street–inspired fashions of the late 1960s and then to the contemporary fashions of today. Mattel maintains a huge design staff that keeps Barbie au courant at any time. Designing a costume for Barbie has become a coup for high-end fashion designers; more than seventy major couturiers have created clothes for Barbie, and more than 150 designers claim her as inspiration (including Tony Award–winning costume designer Gregg Barnes, who has said it was a childhood dream come true when he designed the costume for *Barbie Live in Fairytopia*).

For a woman of her generation, Barbie's résumé is impressive indeed. She's had more than 110 careers—including that of yoga teacher, air force pilot, chef, paleontologist, photographer, news anchor, scuba diver, and computer engineer. She's run for president twice and been to the moon. She has lived in more than 150 countries, and the Barbie brand has consistently generated global revenues of more than $3 billion annually.

But her career is far from over. If the past is prologue, she will continue to adapt to and reflect the world around her, even as she reaches what would be her golden years, were she not eternally a teen. As long as young girls continue to fantasize about what they will be when they grow up, the Barbie doll will be there to help them play out those dreams.

Chatty Cathy 1959

In 1959, the talking doll was not a completely new phenomenon. There had been dolls that said "Mama" if you held them at a precise angle and then didn't budge. But these were clunky and often malfunctioned. As far back as the nineteenth century there had been dolls with a literal phonograph record built into them (Thomas Edison even got involved in making them). But they didn't work very well, either, and they cost a whopping $10, or about $255 in 2013 dollars.

Chatty Cathy, however, was the first *working and affordable* talking doll. Unlike her predecessors, she could be picked up and played with while she talked. Chatty Cathy was chatty indeed, and, at the mere pull of a string (which would activate a small record sewn inside her), could say as many as eleven different things, including "Let's play house," "Please change my dress," "Tell me a story," "Please take me with you," "I hurt myself," and, of course, that staple phrase of talking dolls then

and now: "I love you." (In versions made after 1963, she got even more talkative, adding seven new phrases to her repertoire for a total of eighteen.)

WHY WE LOVED HER BACK

Chatty Cathy was a peer for little girls. She was a best friend *who talked*! She wasn't a baby who had to be taken care of; she was a playmate who could share all the dreams and adventures that little girls imagined. It was the talking that created her special magic. When Mom, a sister, or a best friend wasn't around to play house or say "I love you" . . . Cathy was.

But Cathy was more than just a chatterbox. She was also tremendously fashionable; over the years, her chic wardrobe was continually expanded. Plus, Mattel eventually made versions of the doll with different hair and eye colors—even an African American version—so little girls of all colorings could have Cathys that looked more like "Mom."

DID YOU KNOW?

Cathy's original voice was recorded by June Foray, who was also the voice of Rocky the Flying Squirrel in *Rocky and His Friends/ The Bullwinkle Show,* which was hugely popular at the time. And when Mattel reintroduced the doll in 1970, the voice was none other than Maureen McCormick's— known to a new generation of kids as Marcia Brady from *The Brady Bunch.* (McCormick appeared in commercials for the doll, too.) The 1970 doll was completely redesigned and looked very little like the original.

WHERE IS SHE NOW?

Chatty Cathy was one of the most popular dolls of all time, despite the fact that she had a lot of competition, even during the peak of her popularity from the early to mid-1960s. Ideal's Betsy Wetsy and Tiny Tears were big rivals for young girls' affections, with their gimmicks such as growing hair and magically appearing makeup (which gave rise to what today is called, at least in the toy industry, "the feature doll").

But for all these bells and whistles, the doll that ultimately edged out Chatty Cathy was the womanly yet mute Barbie, who had also been introduced in 1959. What did Barbie have that Cathy didn't? Among other "endowments," Barbie allowed the child to imagine ways the dolls could play *with one another;* play wasn't limited to just Cathy and the child.

As dolls go, Cathy still has a small but loyal collector following. But while she can still be found online and at antiques shops, it's very rare to find a Chatty Cathy that still talks. Whether it's a broken pull string or a disintegrated rubber band that once turned on her speech unit, Chatty Cathy's parts are virtually impossible to repair or replace. Sadly, many of the existing Cathys don't have a lot to say anymore.

They say the maternal bond is one that can't be broken. Perhaps that explains why Chatty Cathy dolls still hold a special place in the hearts of women who grew up in the 1960s and '70s, who still fondly remember Cathy as their first best friend.

Liddle Kiddles 1966

The 1960s were an era of huge innovation and change in the doll business. Today, so-called minidolls are common toys, but in 1966, when Mattel introduced the diminutive Liddle Kiddles, there was nothing like them around.

Liddle Kiddles were dolls that were supposed to be real little kids, just like the kids who played with them. But rather than being role models, like Barbie, or babies to nurture and mother, these dolls were intended to be a kid's peers. And unlike Chatty Cathy, who was one best friend, the Liddle Kiddles were a gang of buddies—just like kids had in their neighborhoods.

There were twenty-four dolls in the original collection, and they stood on average only about three inches tall. The soft, plastic bodies could be shaped into different poses, thanks to a wire armature inside.

The dolls all had names that rhymed —however forced the rhyme was— with "Kiddle." The winter doll, for example, was "Freezy Sliddle." The bedtime doll was "Beddy Bye Biddle." And so forth. There was even a boy doll, "Howard 'Biff' Boodle."

WHY WE LOVED THEM

The dolls were inexpensive and had lots of different accessories, and their hair could be combed and styled—fixing hair always being an important component of doll play. The dolls also came with storybooks that chronicled the fictional adventures of the various Kiddles, while promoting collectibility at the same time.

Based on the success of the originals, Mattel soon extended the line to include Storybook Kiddles, animal Kiddles, and different special dolls for the holidays, including Easter, which was becoming a toy-purchasing period of the year, and, of course, Christmas.

WHERE ARE THEY NOW?

One of the problems with the Liddle Kiddles was always with the wire armature. Too much play would wear out the plastic exterior, and the wires would poke through. So when Polly Pocket, who was not only made entirely of plastic but came with her own protective shell, came along in 1989, she quickly became the miniature doll of choice.

Today the original Liddle Kiddles can still be found in online auctions, and there are rumors that a small company is trying to bring the originals back.

Beautiful Crissy 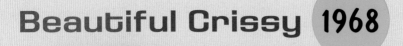 1968

Thanks to the success of Barbie, by the end of the 1960s, there was a huge and growing market for teenage dolls.

What was unique about Crissy, however, was her hair—which could actually "grow," allowing little girls to style her tresses over and over in many different ways. Her flowing red locks, which could reach her feet when fully extended, were operated by a dial on the back of the doll, and would spool or unspool depending on which direction the dial was turned.

CHANGE THE LENGTH OF CRISSY'S HAIR WITHOUT BATTERIES

Beautiful CRISSY

To Mother:

WHY WE LOVED HER

While she wasn't the first doll with growing hair, Crissy was the first to be broadly advertised on television, and many kids remember singing along with the commercial: *Beautiful Crissy has beautiful hair that grows.*

She was such a hit that over the next several years, her parent company, Ideal, introduced new styles and even a friend for Crissy named Velvet. Ideal also introduced versions of Crissy who could move and pose in different ways, such as the 1972 Look Around Crissy with a swiveling waist and a pull-string-activated turning head, allowing girls to imagine that she was just like the real women on the famous Breck shampoo commercials.

WHERE IS SHE NOW?

Crissy, Velvet, and, later, Tressy, were popular throughout the 1970s (there was even a Baby Crissy, a large-sized doll on the scale of Tiny Tears or Thumbelina who became a huge hit in 1973), but were soon superseded by Pretty Cut 'n Grow, a doll with yarn hair that kids could cut, in the late '70s, and Playskool's Dolly Surprise, with her growing ponytail, in the late '80s. For as big as they were, Crissy and gang remain collector's items today.

Beautiful CRISSY

with hair that grows and grows and grows

CREATE A NEW CRISSY WHENEVER YOU LIKE

Baby Alive (1973)

There was nothing new about the drink-and-wet doll by the early 1970s. Betsy Wetsy—who could "drink" water in one end and, well, you know what on the other—had been a staple since 1935 and had even inspired other dolls, such as the lesser-known Dy-Dee doll.

But drink and eat and wet *and poop* . . . now there was an innovation. And it dovetailed perfectly with little girls' age-appropriate fascination with their bodies and natural processes. Targeted at young girls around the age of, or having just completed, toilet training, Baby Alive occupied a very natural place in the child's consciousness and world.

WHY WE LOVED HER

Baby Alive drank regular water from her bottle, and she ate special food that looked like strained peas. The mechanism in the doll pushed the fluid and the solid through a tube until the inevitable happened, and the miniature mommy was required to make a diaper change.

Baby Alive also moved and made baby sounds, so little girls got a fairly complete mommy experience. Though this level of realism was a bit controversial, little girls loved the doll because it allowed them to play the role of the grown-ups who knew that diapers were "for babies"—and they certainly weren't that anymore! So, adult objections or no, Baby Alive became the top-selling doll of 1973.

Baby Alive needed to be cleaned out regularly to keep operating, and there are many stories about little girls who, having run out of the food included with the doll, tried feeding her all kinds of real food . . . and the results weren't pretty. There are tales, too, of the nefarious ways boys played with their sisters' Baby Alive dolls, like feeding them clothesline, pulling it taut from the other end, and watching in hysterics while Baby Alive chewed her way across the line. Tears and time in the corner to "think about what you've done" generally followed.

WHERE IS SHE NOW?

Novelty dolls such as Baby Alive generally have a life span of only a

couple of years, but when Kenner relaunched the doll in 1990 to a new generation of girls, it was just as popular as it was the first time around. Despite its very basic and, by the early '90s, primitive function, the new version sold more than nine million dolls.

Rub-a-Dub Dolly 1973

One of the things that most hit toys have in common is that they "break the rules." In the early 1970s, lots of dolls were breaking the rules. They had to in order to keep up with the fierce competition in the doll market, as dueling companies fought to capture a coveted spot on little girls' wish lists.

Breaking rules was big in 1973. That was the year that Baby Alive broke the rule that you can't feed your dolls food. With that dolly Rubicon crossed, it probably shouldn't have been surprising that it was also the year another taboo was shattered: You can't take your dolls in the bathtub.

WHY WE LOVED HER

Rub-a-Dub Dolly was a watertight plastic doll, designed specifically to be taken into the tub. Parents loved it because it put an end to temper tantrums at bath time (or tragedies when a non-submersible dolly took a dunk). Little girls were delighted that now when they went into the bath, their dolls could come, too.

Rub-a-Dub Dolly also had a tugboat shower (sold separately, of course) so she could float up-

I make bathtime more fun!

sold it was novelty —and perhaps also the commercial, an infectious tune with a silly rhyme that caused many an earworm when the doll was launched:

You give her a bath when you're in the tub.
A bath's so much fun with rub-a-dub-dub.

That pretty much says it all.

WHERE IS SHE NOW?

Unlike Baby Alive, Rub-a-Dub Dolly really didn't do anything other than not get ruined when submerged in the tub, so once Ideal stopped advertising it, the sales dried up, so to speak.

Tyco reintroduced the doll in 1990, but her new tub time was comparatively short, so for the most part the toy lives on in our memories—and the commercial lives on on YouTube, where nostalgic adults can hum along.

right in the tub and rinse off above the surface while little girls got clean.

In all honesty, there really wasn't anything special about this doll. What

Cabbage Patch Kids
1976 and 1983

Ah, they began innocently enough . . . as these things often do. In 1976, artist Xavier Roberts made dolls by hand and sold them at local craft fairs to pay for his college tuition. But, as his story went, these weren't just some ordinary dolls; they were Little People, and kids didn't just own them; they adopted them.

WHY WE LOVED THEM

This twist on the classic narrative of doll acquisition was enough to make them so popular that in 1980, Roberts started a full-fledged manufacturing operation out of a refurbished medical office in Cleveland, Georgia. He named the place Babyland General Hospital. Since Fisher-Price owned the name Little People, Roberts needed a new name, and in a weird burst of inspiration, decided to try to sell the idea of children coming from the cabbage patch. (When you think about it, this fiction made just about as much sense as the notion of children coming from the stork.) At Babyland General, kids could see their soon-to-be adopted dolls "born" in an elaborately staged vegetable garden. Thus, they were aptly named Cabbage Patch Kids.

This small operation started to attract big attention, and parents all over the United States soon clamored to get their hands on one of the dolls while they were still one of a kind. But in 1983 an unlikely suitor—the toy company Coleco, previously known for its air-hockey tables—came calling, bought up the rights, and began to produce the first mass-market Cabbage Patch Kids. Cleverly recognizing that much of the dolls' appeal was the fact that each one was different, just like every real child, Coleco figured out a way to make each doll unique by varying everything from eye color to hair to clothing. Extending the narrative even farther, when children sent in proof of adoption, the doll would get a personalized card on its first birthday.

Little did Coleco's executives know that by Christmas 1983, they wouldn't be able to "grow" enough Cabbage Patch Kids to keep up with the surging demand. As the holidays

approached and Coleco's "patches" began to run dry, panics began to erupt in the aisles of toy stores. Stories of fistfights over the toys made the news, and some determined parents even flew to Europe or Asia to adopt Cabbage Patch Kids, some on the black market and some from legitimate stores in countries where the craze hadn't hit.

Due in part to all this media exposure, Cabbage Patch Kids were the first of the major toy fads of the 1980s and '90s to completely

sweep the culture. And it wasn't just among kids; the fantasy of having a unique baby was so seductive that some adults took to treating them as though they were real, adopted children!

The Cabbage Patch craze shattered another cultural taboo. For the first time, boys found the fantasy of parenthood appealing, and many parents bought the dolls for their young sons. Boys adopting dolls? The world was certainly changing.

WHERE ARE THEY NOW?

By the time that first generation of Cabbage Patch Kids neared their third or fourth birthdays, the craze died down, Coleco went into bankruptcy, and the orphaned Cabbage Patch Kids were in search of a home. Eventually, Mattel took them over and tried to bring them back to life with special fifteenth anniversary dolls, but it seemed the magic was gone. That is, until QVC started selling collectible editions, which became a hit with women in their twenties and thirties—now with real kids at home—who longed to be reunited with their long-lost adopted sons and daughters The brand has changed hands many times, and as the dolls' thirtieth birthday approaches, current owner Jakks Pacific is planning to reintroduce new versions of the original dolls that started it all.

Strawberry Shortcake
1979

She was born in 1977 as a drawing on a line of cards from American Greetings. But by 1979 she had leaped off the paper to become a bona fide three-dimensional toy sensation.

WHY WE LOVED HER

The original Strawberry Shortcake, and her cat, Custard, were, of course, scented (advances in plastics technology in the late 1970s allowed the fragrance to be embedded in the doll and last for a long time), and that was a big part of their charm. As any mom who has caught her young daughter experimenting with her perfume will attest, little girls love scents, and these dolls were no exception. In fact, young girls were so enthralled by this fragrant doll and her feline companion that Strawberry Shortcake's world quickly grew to more than thirty characters, each one scented like her eponymous dessert—Apple Dumplin', Raspberry Tart, Huckleberry Pie, Angel Cake, and so forth—and each with an accompanying pet. A fad quickly ensued.

DID YOU KNOW?
Raspberry Tart was eventually renamed Raspberry Torte, presumably so the little girl wouldn't get—perish the thought!—a reputation.

Part of the appeal of Strawberry and her gang was how cute they were, and she is remembered for ushering in a decade of cuteness in the toy world, paving the way for some of the biggest hits of the 1980s, including Rainbow Brite, Rose Petal Place, My Little Pony, and the Care Bears. Thanks to her large cast of characters, she also established girls' collectibles as a category in its own right. (Ironically, collectible dolls—or as they were more euphemistically named, action figures—had been popular among boys for years.)

WHERE IS SHE NOW?

Strawberry Shortcake toys—and books and TV shows and related items—continued to be popular well into the early 1980s. At the height of Strawberry fever, more than twenty-five million dolls and thirty-five million accessories were sold. But by the middle of the decade, the sweet smell of success finally started to wear off, and by 1985 the toys were out of production.

Still, a strong whiff of nostalgia for Strawberry Shortcake remained in the air, and over the years, different manufacturers have attempted to bring Strawberry back, though these later adaptations haven't been as popular as the originals. The first versions are in the hands of loyal collectors, some of whom claim they can still perceive a faint trace of fragrance.

My Little Pony 1982

Horses. Long, flowing hair. Bright colors. Glitter. More glitter. Put any two of these together and you may have a decent concept for a girls' toy. Put them all together, and you're likely to have a hit. That's exactly what Hasbro did in the early 1980s with the introduction of the My Little Pony line. Its success gave an entirely new meaning to the concept of a "stable" brand.

Girls have always loved horses. *National Velvet*, *My Friend Flicka*, and similar movies have delighted for generations, and the classic literature for young girls is full of horse stories. Barbie had a horse, and over the years there have been many different model and toy horses for little girls to play with and display.

WHY WE LOVED THEM

But My Little Ponies weren't just toy horses for a girl to love. They were an entire universe of horses who acted just like humans—and yet no actual humans were allowed.

Hasbro's first line of six My Little Pony dolls in 1982 were named Blue Belle, Butterscotch, Cotton Candy, Minty, Blossom, and Snuzzle, each with different markings of her hindquarters. The horses weren't soft or cuddly—they were made out of vinyl—but that only seemed to enhance their appeal.

For the next few years, My Little Pony was win, place, and show with little girls. They inspired a movie, a TV show, and as women who remember their avid collector days will recall, all kinds of pony paraphernalia, ranging from socks and T-shirts to pens, notebooks, and Trapper Keeper folders.

Over the next ten years, the pony world kept growing, and My Little Pony soon came in a variety of shapes and sizes—unicorns, flying horses, princesses, brides, baby ponies, rainbow ponies, and so forth—each with a magical, whimsical name. As the line grew, the prevailing logic was that if something could be part of a little girl's play-time fantasy, it could be a pony . . . and indeed it could.

WHERE ARE THEY NOW?

My Little Pony continues to inspire imaginative play among young girls, thanks to new adventures, entertainment, and a continually expanding product line. My Little Pony also has a huge nostalgic following among women who grew up in the 1980s. Perhaps the most unexpected development in the world of My Little Pony fans, however, has been the emergence of a relatively small, but passionate, band of male collectors, mostly in their thirties, who call themselves "Bronies" and who (unironically) share their love of all things My Little Pony both online and at conventions.

Care Bears 1983

What was it about the early 1980s that inspired so much sweetness? The Care Bears first appeared on greeting cards in 1981. Two years later, they had graduated to the world of plush toys. They were originally introduced as "Roly-poly little bears who live high in a land of rainbows and fluffy clouds called Care-a-lot" and who "regularly come to earth to make humans feel better and help them share their feelings with others."

WHY WE LOVED THEM

Their sweetness (bordering on saccharine) reflected the popular taste for the touchy-feely pervading the culture at this time, but instead of running for the insulin (or the ipecac), humans all over the world went running for the Care Bears, and they couldn't get enough. And it wasn't just kids; the Care Bears phenomenon touched people of all ages. There was a bear for virtually any occasion you could think of—and they came in all the colors of the rainbow (the blue Grumpy Bear was the lone exception, a wonderful antidote to all the sugar). And,

in the very '80s spirit of gender neutrality, the Care Bears appealed to many boys as well. As the thinking went, everyone could use a hug from time to time.

Like any successful species, these roly-poly bears were soon re-producing like rabbits. Soon Care Bears cousins came along, repre-senting many corners of the animal kingdom, including—you guessed it—rabbits.

The Care Bears starred in two full-length movies and their own TV show, which ran for two years with more than seventy episodes.

WHERE ARE THEY NOW?

After a whopping forty million toys were sold, the Care Bears' popularity inevitably waned, their work of mak-ing humans feel better and helping them share their feelings with others presumably done. But then, in 2002, a whole new generation arrived from the land of Care-a-lot, and in turn a whole new generation of Care Bears fans was born.

Today, Care Bears toys can still be found on store shelves, largely unchanged from their original look.

Parents enjoy sharing them with their kids. And, like many toys of the 1980s, they have a huge kitsch appeal as well. For those who take their nostalgia a little more seriously, there are also fervent fan sites devoted to the bears, and the original toys are highly prized collectibles.

Rainbow Brite 1983

In the cavalcade of cuteness that ushered in the 1980s, Rainbow Brite joined the Care Bears and Strawberry Shortcake in bringing sweetness to little girls' lives.

But where the bears brought hugs and Strawberry came bearing fruit, Rainbow Brite was all about color. The backstory began with Wisp, an orphan (it's always best in these stories to get the parents out of the way) who was transported to a colorless world. But once Wisp befriended Starlite, a horse with a rainbow tail, releasing the seven Color Kids from captivity, Wisp magically became Rainbow Brite, now with the responsibility to care for all the color on Earth. It was a big job, but this little girl—with her attendant sprites—was up to the challenge.

Though an adult might look at this unlikely tale as excessively cloying, children ate it up, and the toys were a huge hit, in part thanks to the popular TV show that ran from 1984 to 1986.

WHEN DID THE COLORS FADE?

Rainbow Brite proved to have less staying power than some of the other dolls that debuted in this period, and like many a rainbow she soon faded into a memory, though one cherished by many.

There were various attempts to revive the character in 1996, for the twentieth anniversary of the toys in 2004, and again for the twenty-fifth in 2009, but they never found the formula to make her shine again.

WHERE IS SHE NOW?

As the generation who loved her grew up and discovered irony, poor Rainbow had a rough time of it. More than almost any other character of the period, Rainbow Brite has become fodder for parody. The Cartoon Network show *Robot Chicken,* for one, has taken special delight in trashing the character.

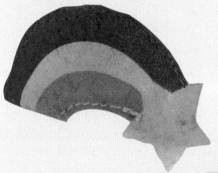

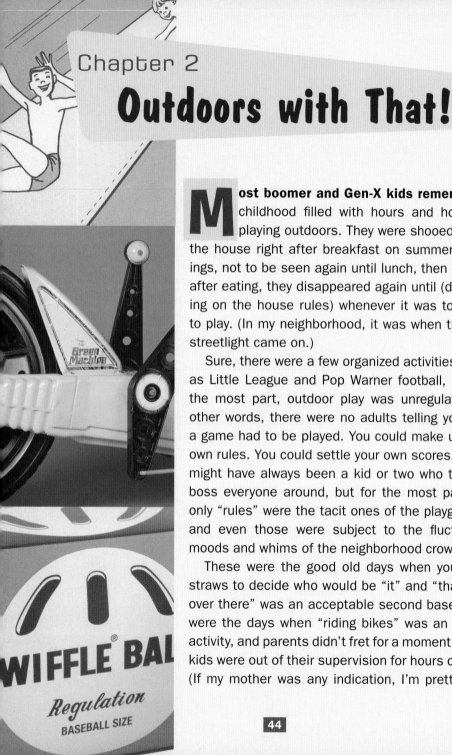

Chapter 2
Outdoors with That!

Most boomer and Gen-X kids remember a childhood filled with hours and hours of playing outdoors. They were shooed out of the house right after breakfast on summer mornings, not to be seen again until lunch, then dinner; after eating, they disappeared again until (depending on the house rules) whenever it was too dark to play. (In my neighborhood, it was when the one streetlight came on.)

Sure, there were a few organized activities, such as Little League and Pop Warner football, but for the most part, outdoor play was unregulated. In other words, there were no adults telling you how a game had to be played. You could make up your own rules. You could settle your own scores. There might have always been a kid or two who tried to boss everyone around, but for the most part the only "rules" were the tacit ones of the playground, and even those were subject to the fluctuating moods and whims of the neighborhood crowd.

These were the good old days when you drew straws to decide who would be "it" and "that rock over there" was an acceptable second base. They were the days when "riding bikes" was an all-day activity, and parents didn't fret for a moment if their kids were out of their supervision for hours on end. (If my mother was any indication, I'm pretty sure

WIFFLE BAL

Regulation

BASEBALL SIZE

they preferred it.) These were the days when kids didn't wear helmets or protective gear. Sure, there were the inevitable spills and scrapes, but serious injuries were rare—and often considered a badge of honor, particularly if a cast was involved. Outdoors was a kid's world, and with it came a sense of freedom that powered play and self-reliance, and created lifelong relationships—and memories.

It was a time unlike today, when many parents would cringe to think of their kids speeding down the sidewalk on a Big Wheel, or throwing themselves onto a wet plastic sheet and sliding with abandon across the lawn. But if those same parents harken back to their own childhoods, they'll remember how outdoor games, played without rules, out from under the watchful gaze of parents and other grown-ups, provided a sense of excitement we all craved.

Probably the most popular and enduring outdoor toy introduced in this period was the Frisbee. At the same time, many people recall hours upon hours of fun spent clocking hops on the Skip-It, or organizing backyard games of Wiffle ball, or putting the Super Ball's amazing bouncing powers to the test.

Today, when getting—or keeping—kids active has become a cultural obsession (thanks in part to the movement to fight childhood obesity, spearheaded by First Lady Michelle Obama) and much of kids' lives are being increasingly taken up with music lessons and language classes and other organized indoor activities, it's worth looking back at a time when active play was an everyday occurrence and the outdoors was a kid's world, limited only by the boundaries of the imagination.

Wiffle Ball 1953

During the 1950s the pickup baseball game was a staple of neighborhood play. Yet rare was the kid who had a regulation baseball, and using hardballs in a backyard game was a risky gambit, since any kid who watched the television shows of the period knew what happened when the ball went through the window of the meany next door. Kids tried to play ball with golf balls and tennis balls, and city kids played stickball with pink Spaldeen balls, but none of these really worked very well. Some toy makers made blow-molded (hollow) balls that looked like baseballs, but they couldn't be pitched. What was a kid to do?

Then came the Wiffle ball. According to Wiffle.com, one day, while watching his son and his friends play, David N. Mullany, who had been a college and semipro pitcher, realized that no plastic ball could be pitched like a baseball, especially when it came to curveballs.

After experimenting with different materials, Mullany found that a ball made out of a thicker plastic and injection molded (made in two pieces) rather than blow-molded

(inflated), with eight oblong holes along the surface, worked the best. Mullany patented his creation and borrowed some money, and he was in business.

Exactly how it works and why it works are still a mystery, according to the company (for more information, see Wiffle.com/welcome.asp). All we know is that it transformed backyard ball forever.

WHERE IS IT NOW?

Over the years, many companies have come up with toy baseballs, but none of them ever worked as well as the original Wiffle ball. It could be a combination of the placement of the holes in the imitators or the cheapness of their plastic, but most of these have been relegated to preschoolers.

The company has branched out into bats, and, naturally, to logo merchandise. The company is private, so we don't know how many units are sold every year, but the classic Wiffle ball is still the best toy baseball on the market.

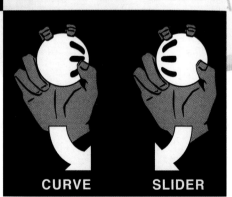

WIFFLE® BALL

Regulation BASEBALL SIZE

IT CURVES!
BAT IT! BOUNCE IT!
SAFE ANYWHERE

IT'S EASY TO THROW CURVES WITH

WIFFLE® BALL

CURVE   SLIDER

Frisbee 1957

As with many hit toys, the story of the Frisbee's origin is surrounded by legend. Flying disks have been used as playthings, sporting goods, and even weapons since the days of the ancients. But by most accounts the invention of the modern-day Frisbee was inspired by a bunch of Yale students who made a game out of tossing empty pie plates to avoid studying. The pies came from the Frisbie Baking Company in Bridgeport, Connecticut.

But empty pie plates were not the most aerodynamic of instruments and so, in 1948, Walter Frederick Morrison developed a plastic version that would fly like a saucer and not wobble through the air like, well, a pie plate. He named it the Pluto Platter to capitalize on the public's then-current fascination with outer space and aliens, and sold it mostly through demonstrations and on college campuses. It was only a modest success.

That is, until 1955, when Morrison teamed up with Arthur "Spud" Melin and Richard Knerr, who had just formed the now-legendary company Wham-O and were marketing their first product—a slingshot. Together, they patented and began to produce and market what we would today recognize as a Frisbee. (Knerr, by the way, is credited with renaming the toy Frisbee, a phonetic spelling of the name of the pie company—and one that wouldn't infringe on any trademark.)

WHY WE LOVED IT

The Frisbee wasn't originally marketed as a toy; it was billed as a sport, which, of course, meant that

DID YOU KNOW?

Even dogs found their way into the Frisbee sports world. The first Frisbee-catching dog was Ashley Whippet, who put the sport—one that now has national championships—on the map. (In the 1980s, yours truly accompanied some of these canine athletes to exhibitions at most of the major professional baseball stadiums in the United States, and I can tell you that fans of dog Frisbee take it no less seriously than fans of any other professional sport.)

it wasn't just for kids. Soon after its introduction, the Frisbee became a fixture in parks, on beaches, and virtually anywhere adults and kids alike could play the new game.

The Frisbee didn't necessarily lend itself to a lot of innovation or product enhancements, but as both its popularity and the level of competition grew, in 1964, Wham-O cleverly introduced the first "professional" Frisbee, which was larger and heavier than the original and, thus, demanded a bit more skill. These professional models were a sleek black and white; the "toy" versions were still produced in a rainbow of colors. A glow-in-the-dark version that could be played at night (and could easily be recharged by placing it over the headlight of a car) was also a hit.

For those unsatisfied with simple throw and catch, Frisbee soon inspired a number of spin-off sports.

Ultimate Frisbee, a combination of football, baseball, and soccer using the disks, came on the scene in 1967, and Frisbee golf, which involved walking a field, trying to toss the disks into Frisbee-sized "golf" holes—chain baskets hanging from metal poles—soon followed, and actually became a recognized sport.

Slip 'N Slide 1961

If ever there was a toy that was feared and loved in equal measure, it was the Slip 'N Slide. Naturally kids were enamored of the toy that let them fly across the lawn on a sheet of plastic. Cautious parents, on the other hand, saw only the potential danger. As so often happens in these kinds of things, though, the kids generally won out, and soon the world was divided between those kids who had a Slip 'N Slide and those who were forbidden to play on it.

But whether you had one or not, for most kids the Slip 'N Slide completely transformed backyard play. Sure, kids had been running under the lawn sprinkler for years as a way of cooling off, and wading pools had been around since the rise of the suburbs at the end of World War II, but the Slip 'N Slide brought outdoor water play to a whole new level.

WHY WE LOVED IT

The toy was nothing more than a long sheet of yellow plastic that had a perforated tube running alongside it. You connected the garden hose to one end of the tube, and a shower of water kept the plastic sheet nice and slippery wet. Kids ran, threw themselves down, and slid all the way to the end. It was like having a water slide in your own backyard.

Obviously, placement of the slide was everything. Adults will surely recall all the time spent scouring the yard for the perfect spot, ideally on a downhill slant with no rocks or twigs underneath. The slide preferably shot you out onto the lawn a good distance from the sidewalk.

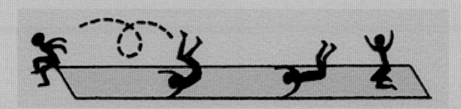

Despite the per-ceived dangers, injuries were few and far between, unless you count the fights that ensued over whose turn it was.

WHERE IS IT NOW?

The Slip 'N Slide has never lost its appeal—even to modern-day kids—and fifty years later, it's still on the market. Of course, today's versions have gotten more and more sophisticated, some resembling veritable backyard water parks, with everything from tunnels to slides that end in pools. Still, there's no question that the simple action of sliding across the lawn on a thin sheet of plastic is still the thrill kids love. If only, many have lamented, they made a version for adults.

Jingle Jump 1964, Lemon Twist 1976, and Skip-It c.1987

Jumping rope—and all its variations—is a game almost as old as civilization itself. Wherever kids have had a piece of rope and a little ingenuity, games followed. The Dutch brought jump rope when they came to the New World, and while for many years the fun required a simple piece of rope, in the 1960s industrious toy makers saw an opportunity in making and marketing clever variations on the classic game.

One of the first of these mass-produced toys was the Jingle Jump, which, thanks to the low one-dollar retail price and an infectious TV commercial, quickly became a huge hit. The toy was composed of a long plastic cord with a hollow ball on one end and a piece that fastened around the heel of a shoe on the other.

HOW WE PLAYED WITH IT

The idea was to attach the Jingle Jump to one foot, then bend over, pick up the ball and toss it in front of you, and swing the foot to get it spinning. Then you would hop over the cord as the ball went around and around—as many times as you could before the device lost momentum, or you tripped up. Oh, and a small box on the back had a bell inside that—you guessed it—jingled while you jumped. It wasn't easy, but that was part of the fun, as kids spent hours upon hours trying to beat their record number of hops, and the toy became a kind of minifad for a season.

As tends to happen, success breeds imitation, and soon a similar item called Footsie hit the market. Only instead of the heel contraption, Footsie had a ring that slipped around the ankle. Originally, Footsie had a bell at the end of its cord, but that was changed to a ball later on. Either way, it was certainly easier to use, and kids loved it.

Then in the mid-1970s, Chemtoy replaced the simple ball with a plastic lemon, used green plastic for the ring and cord, and renamed the toy Lemon Twist. Though the toy worked the exact same way as the original, this stylistic tweak was enough to create a whole new minicraze.

Better players quickly learned that the secret to a higher number of jumps was to get a rocking motion going as they shifted their feet—a kind of forward and back hop. Real experts could go almost as long as their stamina held out.

WHERE IS IT NOW?

Sadly, by the late 1970s, as video games became an exciting new novelty and kids began spending more and more of their playtime indoors, outdoor games like this fell out of favor. But it was ultimately new safety regulations that brought about the Jingle Jump's demise. For one, no toy could have a cord more than twelve inches long because of the risk that it could wrap around a child's neck and strangle them—which was a bit of a problem—unless the manufacturers created breakaway cords.

However, in the late 1980s Tiger Electronics solved that problem by replacing the cord with a hollow plastic rod. They renamed the toy Skip-It, and it became an instant hit. Once again, TV advertising played a huge role in inspiring a new generation of kids to hop to it. Later versions included an electronic counter in the ball, which had the added bonus of resolving many a playground dispute over who had racked up the most hops.

In 2013, the toy is coming back in all sorts of newfangled incarnations, including basic reproductions of the classic toys and the fancier Twister Rave Skip-It, a glow-in-the-dark version that lights up in neon colors as you skip.

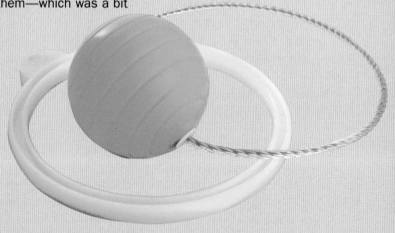

Super Ball 1965

In 1965, the biggest fad of the year was the Super Ball. Yes, it may have looked like just a basic ball, but it had super bouncing powers. Made of a highly compressed synthetic rubber (with the appropriately space age name Zectron) developed by chemist Norman Stingley, and marketed by Wham-O, the Super Ball could leap over a three-story house and shoot back up when dropped from a building, and, if you hurled it in a small room, it would ricochet off the walls for what seemed like a good long time.

WHY WE LOVED IT

Perhaps it was the classic appeal of anything that seems to defy physics and logic. Or maybe it was just cool how high the thing bounced. Either way, with the United States in the midst of a space race and enamored of things that went faster, farther, and higher, the ninety-eight-cent Super Ball was just the ticket. More than seven million of them were sold in their first year on the market.

The first Super Ball was about the size of the famous Pinky ball, also known as the Spaldeen, that had been introduced in the 1940s. Essentially a tennis ball without the fuzz, the Spaldeen had been the gold standard for a rubber ball—that is, until the Super Ball bounced into town.

As fun as it was, the Pinky simply couldn't compete with the Super Ball's special compressed rubber and its incredible elastic properties. Of course, as with any simple toy, imagination was key, and kids delighted in creating all kinds of games and testing Super Ball's potential in all kinds of ways: throwing it out of windows, bouncing it off the roofs of houses, and whacking it with baseball bats, to name just a few. Many of the games included trying to get out of the way of the ball as it went zinging past; it could leave a mark if you got hit with it at full speed. Still, that seemed to be part of the fun as well.

WHERE IS IT NOW?

According to Wham-O, at the height of the craze, they were turning out Super Balls at a rate of approximately 170,000 a day. But as with all superhot fads, the novelty soon cooled off, and by the end of 1966, the Super Ball fad had lost its bounce.

You'd be hard-pressed to find an original 1965 Super Ball these days. Zectron, the synthetic rubber that gave it its bounce, tended to fall apart. Super Balls also were easily lost and sometimes lost chunks when they hit surfaces at great speed.

In 2009, Maui toys introduced the Hyper Charged Sky Ball, a hollow ball about the size of a softball pumped full of a mix of oxygen and helium that could purportedly bounce seventy-five feet in the air. Produced in transparent jewel-like colors, this modern-day Super Ball became a must-have for a new generation of kids.

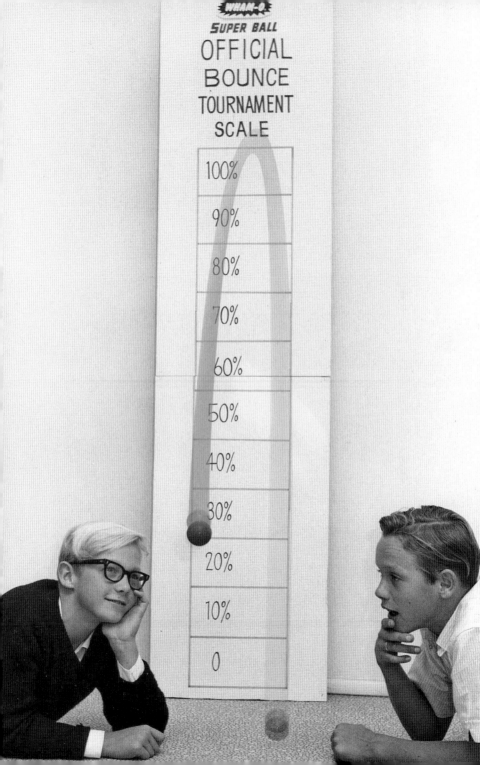

Big Wheel 1969

When Marx introduced the first Big Wheel in 1969—made of blow-molded plastic with the eponymous oversized front wheel and two smaller back wheels—it was a huge success, and the first innovation on the tricycle in, well, ever. Kids sat in a low-slung seat that could be adjusted as they grew.

It was not designed for mechanical efficiency. Sitting down low and leaning back, kids who remember riding it around their neighborhoods recall the effort it took to get the darn thing moving. It took a lot of pushing to get rolling. But once it was on the move the sound of those hollow plastic wheels on pavement was unmistakable.

Kids also loved getting it going and then pulling the handlebars sharply to one side to go into a spin. It felt like being a real daredevil, that's for sure. Parents liked it because it was inexpensive, but they also felt that it was safer than a traditional tricycle, a belief fostered by the Consumer Products Safety Commission.

The look was very much of its time. It's no accident that the movie *Easy Rider* was released the same year, and while many of the kids answering the call of the open sidewalk would not have seen the movie, the sense of freedom and "rebellion" of riding the chopper-like plastic toy certainly added to its cachet.

WHAT HAPPENED?

As so often happens in the toy industry, success breeds knockoffs, and though Marx had trademarked the name "Big Wheel," similar ride-on toys started to flood the market in the early 1970s. By that time, the term "Big Wheel"

had become generic. After Marx declared bankruptcy, Empire bought the name and the molds and produced Big Wheel toys for several years, until they, too, folded. Other types of ride-ons had taken over the market.

WHERE IS IT NOW?

The brand name "Big Wheel" changed hands at least one more time, though it never was relaunched with any kind of success. The toy was inducted into the Strong's National Toy Hall of Fame in 2009, meaning that it was certainly a classic, though at the time it seemed as though it was a toy whose time had passed.

Well, not so fast. In 2012, Kids Only!, a division of Jakks Pacific, acquired the rights. They reintroduced the ride-on in time for the summer season, and a new generation of kids discovered the simple fun of this classic.

As part of their promotion, Kids Only! produced two prototype models of the Big Wheel in a size that a contemporary adult could ride. They proved to be so popular wherever they were shown that for 2014, the company decided to put them into production and sell them for $199—or about the cost of twenty of the originals in 1969.

NERF Ball 1969

How many times throughout your childhood did your mom, her nerves fraying, yell, "Outdoors with that!"? This was often in response to a spirited ball game taking place in the living room, or a near disaster involving your throwing arm and her Hummel figurines. Even

for those of us who grew up with the most lax household rules (whose mothers, like mine, just rolled their eyes at their rambunctious kids), playing ball in the house was definitely verboten. That is, until 1969, when the "world's first official indoor ball" was introduced.

WHY WE LOVED IT

Suddenly, not only *could* kids play basketball, soccer, and even football indoors, they were actually allowed to! Score one for kids; score one for mom; and score many millions for NERF, whose irreverent marketing slogans included "Throw it indoors. You can't hurt babies or old people."

Or course, NERF didn't set out to turn American living rooms into veritable playgrounds. As NERF inventor Reyn Guyer says, "For every great idea, there are usually, oh, several hundred rotten ideas." In 1969, Guyer and his designers were trying to develop a game similar to Twister

The NERF BALL does it all!

(which had been a huge hit for Guyer in 1966), in which players had to avoid stepping on specific squares on a giant game board. To keep other players off the forbidden squares, the designers cut up pieces of foam, which players could then throw at one another. The game itself wasn't particularly fun, but, as the playful designers soon discovered, throwing the pieces of foam at one another was! (When in the history of play has throwing things at other people *not* been fun?)

So Guyer and his team fashioned the foam into orange softball-sized spheres, boxed them up, and shipped them to Parker Brothers, who sold more than four million of them in the first year (a huge departure for Parker Brothers, which had primarily been a board game company).

By the mid-1970s the brand NERF had become synonymous with any type of active plaything that could be marketed under the banner "soft, safe fun." So naturally, that soon came to include "blasters"—which were modeled after various weapons but were plastic, fluorescent, and shot out foam balls. (Parents

NeRF™ ball

SAFE! The Nerf Ball is made of incredibly soft and spongy synthetic foam. Throw it around indoors; you can't damage lamps or break windows. You can't hurt babies or old people.

Parker Brothers
Official
NeRF ball™
The worlds first
INDOOR BALL

and antiviolence advocates who were concerned about children playing with toy guns seemed to have no compunction about handing the little ones a blaster.)

In 1989, Milton Bradley's Blast-A-Ball game was the first to use NERF products as ammunition, and it was an instant hit. After that, the blasters started coming in rapid fires with the dart blaster, the Super Soaker water gun, and the popular NERF Action Blasters Big Bad Bow bow and arrow set, which debuted in 1991. Meanwhile, sports fans could still play ball indoors with NERF night vision footballs or Nerfoop basketball sets.

WHERE IS IT NOW?

Advances in materials helped propel the NERF line into the twenty-first century as their use of more sophisticated, compressed foam allowed their balls and darts and discs to fly faster and farther and hit their targets with nearly military precision—while still leaving mom's souvenir teacup collection unshattered.

Today, increasingly sophisticated blasters are among Hasbro's top sellers, and its legions of fans include kids and adults. NERF was also one of the first brands to embrace social media, building an entire online "NERF Nation."

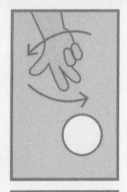

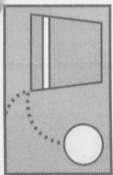

The Green Machine

The Big Wheel was such a hit that kids wanted to ride it forever. There was only one problem: There came that inevitable day when the kid had grown too big. Marx, who had built a huge business on the Big Wheel, didn't want to lose those riders to anything as "ordinary" as a bicycle—perish the thought—and thus came up with the Green Machine.

Designed and promoted for "guys eight, nine, and ten years old who really know how to ride," as the commercial proclaimed, this was the toy for the kids who had outgrown the Big Wheel. Though it was marketed specifically to boys, there were plenty of girls dying to rule the sidewalk with this sleek, low-slung three-wheeled beauty.

WHY WE LOVED IT

What made the Green Machine unique, other than its size, was the steering mechanism. Where the Big Wheel had a traditional tricycle handlebar steering, the Green Machine had two levers that moved the back axle. Like the Big Wheel, it took a lot of effort to get the thing rolling, but once in motion it was more responsive and easier to steer. The showy move was the spin, executed by pushing the levers in opposite directions while leaning into the rotation.

As with the Big Wheel, the low center of gravity virtually assured a tip-proof ride. Moms loved any toy that kept their

eight-to-ten-year-olds—a notoriously daredevil group—actually safer even when executing dramatic spinouts and stunts. (The idea that a kid would need to wear a helmet or other protective gear on this kind of contraption was still many years away.)

WHERE IS IT NOW?

Unlike the Big Wheel, and perhaps because its construction was more sophisticated, the Green Machine was never knocked off the road by other manufacturers.

Today the Green Machine is still made by Huffy, but while the name is the same, it's not the toy you remember. It's still got the lever-based steering, but given Huffy's emphasis on bicycles, it's more like a recumbent bike with rubber tires and a handbrake. They do make a version that will hold a grown-up, though, just in case you want to revisit your former glory days on the sidewalk.

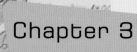

Chapter 3
Batteries Not Included

MR. MACHINE

In books and movies from *The Nutcracker* to *The Velveteen Rabbit* to *Winnie-the-Pooh* (and in more recent years *Toy Story*), children have always been fascinated by the idea that their toys could come to life. After all, the ability to pretend that Baby Alive was really a living, breathing baby, or that King Zor was a living, roaring dinosaur, added a new dimension to play. Well, starting in the mid-1950s, improvements in battery technology finally made it possible—and affordable—to actually breathe life into an inanimate toy.

In the science and engineering-obsessed years after World War II, robots and robotics captured the imagination of adults and children—and in turn, the attention of toy makers. (The term "robot" comes from the 1920 play *R.U.R.* by Carl Capek, in which an army of factory-made artificial people rises up to extinguish the human race.) Early robots such as Mr. Machine, the marching wind-up robot invented by Marvin Glass in 1960, used friction, or primitive wind-up motors. The next generation of robotic toys, however, used batteries—including King Zor, the rampaging dinosaur, Big Loo, the robot with flashing eyes you could switch on and off, and Teddy Ruxpin, the storytelling bear. Batteries even powered board games such as Operation and Fascination, the electric maze race game. However, these toys were clunky, took a lot of battery power (it took four C batteries just to get Teddy talking), and the juice didn't last long. Even into the 1970s, just a few hours of play could drain the batteries, and a toy left unattended for a while was likely to be damaged by leaking batteries.

In 1978, however, Milton Bradley opened a new frontier in electronic toys with Simon, one of the first games where the game play was controlled by a computer chip, and suddenly there was a whole new market—and need for—batteries. The basic pull string of a Chatty Cathy, wind-up mechanisms, or even a child's push suddenly seemed very simplistic as new levels of mechanical magic were powered by the relatively new alkaline batteries.

In today's world, where three-year-olds play on iPads and robots are powered by smaller and smaller microchips, it's easy to forget that it once took a handful of batteries to get a toy to have some rudimentary movements or even light up. And there was always the chance that your batteries would run out while you were playing and you had to pilfer them from another battery-operated appliance in order to keep the action going. Still, as cool as today's high-tech toys are (and as mad as Dad would get when he would find out that—yet again—there were no batteries in the flashlight), back in the day, there were few things more thrilling than the simple delight of flipping a switch and watching a toy come miraculously to life. It was a kind of magic kids had never experienced before.

Mr. Machine 1960

Billed as "the modern take-apart robot with a personality," Mr. Machine was one of the first humanoid robots—a mechanical best friend. Boys who came of age in the 1960s will perhaps remember the thrill of cranking the giant key attached to his back, then marveling as he marched, arms swinging, across the rec room floor. This marvel was designed by Marvin Glass, who went on to become one of the most influential toy designers of the baby boom generation, and it was his first breakthrough hit—after about eleven patient years in the industry. Legend has it that Glass got the idea for Mr. Machine after his wife, in an argument, accused him of being a human machine.

Glass, who had an impressive mastery of mechanics and an uncanny ability to make them work in mass-produced, relatively inexpensive plastic playthings, would go on to create some of the most beloved toys of the twentieth century, including Mystery Date, Time Bomb, Lite-Brite, Rock 'Em Sock 'Em Robots, Operation, Tip It, Toss Across, and many more.

WHY WE LOVED HIM

With gears and cranks that could be seen through his transparent body, Mr. Machine delighted the emerging generation of hobbyists, tinkerers, and science geeks who were fascinated by anything robotic. Featuring an arm-swinging walk, a chomping mouth, a dinging bell, and a siren that rang every fifteen seconds, Mr. Machine was very high-tech indeed for his time.

The popularity of Mr. Machine is in many ways an early example of the power of what we now call viral advertising. In 1960, as Saturday morning television was nearing the peak of its influence, kids everywhere could be heard marching around singing the infectious jingle:

> . . . the greatest toy you've ever
>   seen.
> And his name is Mr. Machine.

(It was so effective that Ideal put an image of Mr. Machine in all of its advertising and on many of its other toy packages over the next several years. Along with the oval Ideal logo, he became inextricably associated with the company.) Parents succumbed to the advertising as well—perhaps to get the kids to stop singing—and Mr. Machine marched into homes nationwide.

Despite the fact that Mr. Machine was a goofy-looking robot, Ideal promoted him as "educational," which made him a little more palatable for parents. (This is a time-honored strategy that seems to work on every generation.) What could kids learn from Mr. Machine? Well, how about engineering? Yeah, that's it. You could take Mr. Machine apart and put

him back together again and learn everything there was to know about gears and machinery. Unfortunately, as those who owned one will recall, getting him back together again wasn't always as easy as it sounded, and it was more a lesson in frustration than engineering. Fortunately for parents, Mr. Machine came fully assembled, and for the most part kids really wanted to just turn the key and watch him on his merry march.

WHERE IS HE NOW?

Mr. Machine had a good run for a couple of years and then marched off into oblivion. At the height of the toy's popularity, Ideal also created a basic board game that used miniature Mr. Machine figures, but this had a limited life.

In 1977, Ideal reissued Mr. Machine in a version that could no longer be disassembled (to appease safety advocates), but he never caught on. Robots had taken on a much more sophisticated mien by that time, and the fact that "the modern take-apart robot," was no longer either modern or able to be taken apart kind of spoiled the fun.

Today, an original Mr. Machine is a treasured find for a small but avid group of collectors, but for many others he is just a happy memory of a simpler time.

KING ZOR the DINOSAUR

IDEAL

(A) KING ZOR
operated toy. Pr
his forked tongu
away, aurns from
in a new directio
when a rubber-tipp
tail, King Zor roars h
in the direction from
He shoots one ball
Finally whe
weakened
is made o
and a quan
loaded in h
batteries. Wt

nosaur Gun
plastic balls are
operates on two D-cell

$20.00

4811/6JT1097 ....

King Zor 1962

King Zor, the rampaging dinosaur, would seem quaint by today's standards, and the one-minute commercial that made him a sensation looks downright dull compared to today's amped-up toy ads. Nonetheless, King Zor was a marvel of mechanical engineering at the time. The blue-green battery-operated dinosaur was thirty-one inches long and was one of the first toys that could actively engage in battle with kids.

HOW WE PLAYED WITH IT

To bring King Zor to life, kids loaded up the launcher on his back with five yellow plastic balls (or "missiles" in Zor's lingo), turned him on, and watched him jerk randomly around. If he bumped into an obstacle with his protruding forked tongue, he would back up and turn a different direction. While the commercial said he was on a "rampage," said rampage was more in the kids' imagination, as Zor was actually fairly benign. However, the intrepid dinosaur hunter could fire suction cup darts from the spring-loaded gun—included with the toy—at King Zor, and if a dart connected with the disc on his tail, King Zor would turn and shoot his missiles at his attacker.

WHERE IS HE NOW?

Marvin Glass designed King Zor as a follow-up to his successful Mr. Machine, but Zor didn't sell as well as Mr. Machine (partially because Mr. Machine appealed to both boys and girls, while—at least in 1962—dinosaur hunting was strictly for boys). As with Mr. Machine, Ideal hoped to launch a character and introduced a Zor board game, but ultimately, Zor lumbered toward extinction after only one season.

Big Loo 1963

I f ever there was a toy that tried to do *everything* that would appeal to boys, it was this three-foot-tall shiny green, red, and gold robot from the toy maker Marx. It was feature-packed from the top of its bullet-shaped head to the wheeled base that stood in for his toes.

WHY WE LOVED HIM

Starting at the top, kids could look—and pretend to take aim at targets—through the scope at the top of his head. They could switch his glowing red eyes on or off. They could talk into the mouthpiece on the back of his head and hear their words in a robotic voice, or get him to say one of ten different phrases with the turn of a crank. His armored chest held two suction cup darts that could be fired from behind. His back was even equipped with a metal tab that could be used as a Morse code clicker (complete with a label for decoding the code).

He had a whistle kids could blow and a bell, and his left arm, which was fixed to his side at a ninety-degree angle, could fire small red balls. His right arm swung freely and had a trigger-operated hand with which Big Loo could pick up objects when he bent at the waist. His left foot held a spring-loaded rocket launcher, and if you turned him over, you would find a compass in his base. Oh, and he squirted water out of his navel.

Kids got all of this for $9.99, which was a lot of money in 1963, but for one glorious holiday season, boys everywhere deemed him worth every penny.

WHERE IS HE NOW?

Big Loo is mostly found in toy museums today. Occasionally one that survived the active play (as you can imagine, Big Loo tended to take quite a beating) will crop up in an online auction. A toy in good working condition can fetch more than $1,000, and the bidding can get very lively. But for most boomers who had Big Loo—or who envied the friend who had him—the memory will have to suffice.

Operation 1965

In the early 1960s, battery-operated games were still a novelty. Then, in 1965, came Operation. The construction was simple. The basic game board was a sheet of cardboard with metal-edged holes cut into it. Sounds thrilling, right? But here's what made it fun: The board was a picture of a patient on a table, and the holes held body parts that needed to be operated on. The "operation" consisted of removing these small plastic body parts from the holes using a pair of attached tweezers. But if the tweezers touched the side of the holes for even a millisecond, the game buzzed loudly, and the patient's nose lit up. Fail.

WHY WE LOVED IT

Of course, this was all in good fun, and the whimsical operations included removing a tiny wrench from the patient's ankle (wrenched ankle), a small piece of bread from the patient's stomach (the breadbasket), and so forth. From the funny bone to the spare ribs to the butterflies

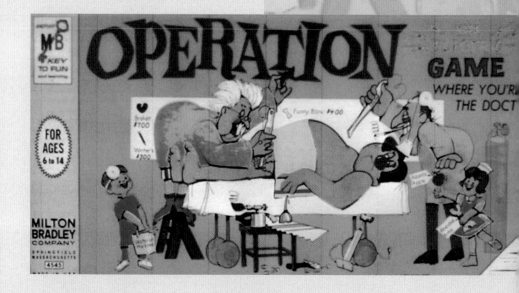

in the stomach to the charley horse (the puns just kept on coming) each piece had a different shape and a different point value. On each turn players drew cards to see what operation they would perform, and if they

WHERE IS IT NOW?

Operation proved to be a major hit, and it quickly became both a classic and a kitsch item, inspiring T-shirts, minigames, and much more.

Many different versions have been introduced over the years, including tie-ins based on popular characters such as Shrek, Spider-Man, *Toy Story*, Iron Man, Lightning McQueen, SpongeBob SquarePants, and Homer Simpson.

But while there have been many patients to grace the operating table, the original character, now called "Cavity Sam," is a pop culture icon.

did it successfully, they kept the plastic piece and the points.

The game was always challenging for little kids, as it required a steady hand and good coordination, but it was also hilarious when the operations didn't go quite as planned.

Simon 1978

As sophisticated as computers are today, it may be hard to believe that there was a time when a "computer-controlled game" could capture the imagination of the culture. But that's what happened when Milton Bradley launched Simon in 1978. The Apple II and Tandy's TRS-80 were only a year old, and the home computer was in its infancy, as was electronic gaming: The Atari 2600 had just made its debut in 1977. This was the brief moment in our culture during which comparatively few people owned computers, yet everyone was fascinated by them, so a handheld game run *by a computer* was about as exciting as it got. It was, quite literally, a game changer.

WHY WE LOVED IT

As jaw dropping as this technology was at the time, however, the play itself was nothing new. It was classic, in fact. The game took its name from the classic kids' game Simon Says, and it was a simple memory game. In fact, Simon's simplicity was part of the secret of its success. Simply mimic the pattern of the flashing lights and sounds until you forget which comes next.

People watched in wonder as the game changed up the patterns and speeds, amping up the challenge with each round. Like the best games, it was easy to play and fun to play over and over, since it was different every time it was played.

WHERE IS IT NOW?

Simon not only ushered in the era of electronic games, it made memory games popular again. It wasn't long before any game with any kind of memory element—and there were a lot of them that followed—was described as a Simon-type game. (They had previously been called Concentration-type games, after the TV show and home game in the 1960s and early '70s.)

Milton Bradley capitalized on the success of the game by introducing the multiplayer Super Simon, which allowed head-to-head competition, and Pocket Simon, for play on the go. As electronics got smaller and smaller, there were even miniature keychain versions.

Today Simon is still made in a variety of versions, and Basic Fun is rein- troducing the original for 2013. Still, like many other electronic games of a simpler era, it now is also an app, a computer game, and an online multiplayer challenge. It just goes to show that while technology is always changing, play patterns stay largely the same.

Teddy Ruxpin 1985

Ever since there have been dolls and stuffed animals, kids have imagined having conversations with them. These best friends are so real to so many kids, it's no wonder they wish they would be able to come to life.

In 1985, that wish came true when Worlds of Wonder introduced Teddy Ruxpin, the first talking storytelling teddy bear.

People had never seen anything like it, and the sensation Teddy caused was epic. He became the bestselling toy of 1985 and 1986. There had been other toys that had incorporated audiocassettes before, but Teddy was especially cool because his eyes and mouth actually moved as the cassette tape in his back played.

He was the next best thing to real, and he caused as much of a stir as the original teddy bear had caused eighty-two years before. Kids didn't even care that Teddy wasn't exactly huggable (his sweatshirt covered a very large and very hard tape recorder—one that took four C batteries, no less). They just loved his stories, which quickly became so popular they inspired his own TV series and an entire line of licensed products.

HOW TEDDY LOST HIS WAY

Teddy Ruxpin made Worlds of Wonder shareholders very rich. However, some bad financial moves ultimately caused the company to collapse with the stock market crash of 1987—and Worlds of Wonder went under. Teddy was acquired by Hasbro and later by Yes! Entertainment, but he was never quite the same.

WHERE IS HE NOW?

As recently as 2005, there have been efforts to bring Teddy Ruxpin out of hibernation, but none has ever taken hold. Still, that hasn't stopped his original fans from keeping the memories alive. Today there

is a sizable Teddy Ruxpin collectible market, and there are legions of websites devoted to keeping Teddy telling stories.

Today, it's hard to find a toy that *doesn't* talk, but people who will always love Teddy Ruxpin will never forget the sheer joy of the first time they asked the bear to "tell me a story"—and he did.

DID YOU KNOW?
One main reason his speech seemed so "natural" (for a talking bear, at least) is because signals that controlled the movements of his mouth and eyes were actually embedded on one track of the audiotape.

THE WORLD OF
TEDDY RUXPIN

Teddy Ruxpin Lullabies
Warm and Cuddly Songs to Dream By

WORLDS OF WONDER

Leota™

Prince Arin™

y What's-It™

Newton Gimmick™

Teddy Ruxpin™

Tweeg™

Gutang™

Grunge™

cess Aruzia™

Grubby™

Fob™

Mudblup™

Bounder™

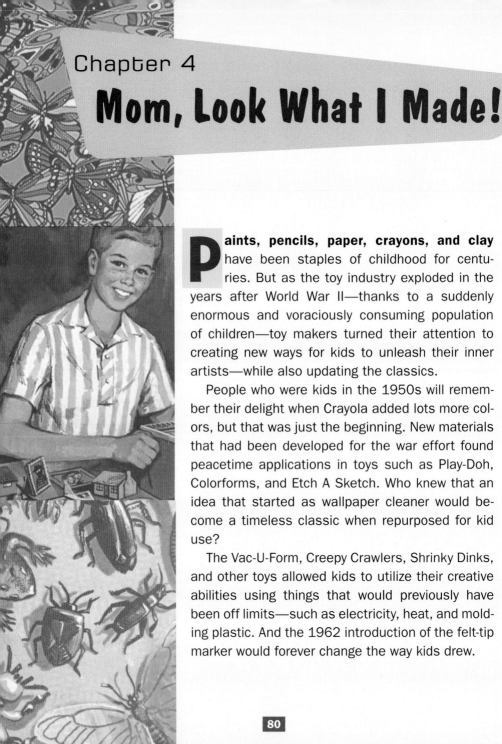

Chapter 4

Mom, Look What I Made!

Paints, pencils, paper, crayons, and clay have been staples of childhood for centuries. But as the toy industry exploded in the years after World War II—thanks to a suddenly enormous and voraciously consuming population of children—toy makers turned their attention to creating new ways for kids to unleash their inner artists—while also updating the classics.

People who were kids in the 1950s will remember their delight when Crayola added lots more colors, but that was just the beginning. New materials that had been developed for the war effort found peacetime applications in toys such as Play-Doh, Colorforms, and Etch A Sketch. Who knew that an idea that started as wallpaper cleaner would become a timeless classic when repurposed for kid use?

The Vac-U-Form, Creepy Crawlers, Shrinky Dinks, and other toys allowed kids to utilize their creative abilities using things that would previously have been off limits—such as electricity, heat, and molding plastic. And the 1962 introduction of the felt-tip marker would forever change the way kids drew.

At the same time, the space race and the cul-turewide focus on science and engineering inspired innovation in "do-it-at-home" art such as the Spi-rograph. The growing emphasis on self-expression and the individual that began to take hold in the 1960s also had a big impact on this category. The magic of every arts and crafts toy was—and still is—that it puts the kid's imagination at the center of the experience.

And part of the fun was wowing your parents with the results. How many moms, for instance, feigned rapture over a colored-in life-size DoodleArt poster, a glowing neon Lite-Brite display, or a (usually ined-ible) brownie conceived in an Easy-Bake Oven?

In a testament to their impact on our memo-ries and our culture, many of these toys are still around today. Even in our technology-driven era of computers and iPads, kids still love arts and crafts projects and the thrill of making something with their own hands. For all their simple fun, these are modes of self-expression that you'll never find in a computer chip. They are powered by that one truly unique energy force—a child's imagination.

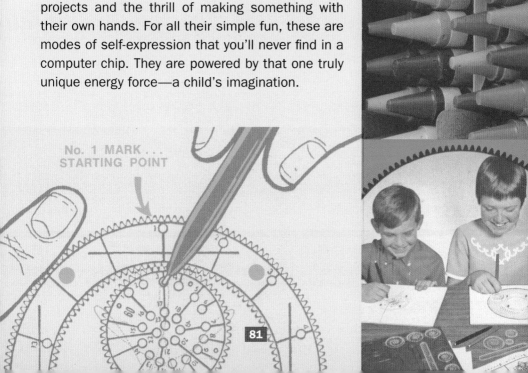

No. 1 MARK...
STARTING POINT

Colorforms 1951

In 1951, two art students named Harry and Patricia Kislevitz were introduced to a lightweight and flexible type of vinyl that a friend was using to manufacture pocketbooks. Once they discovered that this new type of vinyl stuck to the semigloss paint in their bathroom, they began cutting out shapes and decorating with them, even encouraging visitors to add their own cutout creations to the wall.

Seeing how much their dinner guests enjoyed their home-spun art project, Harry and Patricia decided to try to launch it as a product, and created Colorforms:

sets that included basic shapes, letters, and numbers—made of that same vinyl—which could be stuck to a special piece of cardboard finished with a shiny plastic surface. First picked up by the high-end toy retailer FAO Schwarz, the product was sold primarily as an educational toy and was an immediate hit.

WHY WE LOVED IT

The appeal of Colorforms was that they allowed any kid to become an artist. No glue or even scissors were required; the shapes stuck like magic to the board and to each other and could be peeled off just as easily to be reused over and over. Colorforms were among the first toys to be advertised on television, which certainly helped spur demand.

In 1962, Colorforms introduced a doll called Miss Weather, whom kids could dress up, using their Colorforms, in rain slickers, ski jackets, and so on. Thanks to appearances on *Captain Kangaroo,* she became a top seller and helped drive the popularity of the brand.

Given the success of Miss Weather, it wasn't long before Colorforms began creating tie-ins to popular cartoon characters and favorite stories. Over the years, Shari Lewis, Mickey Mouse, *Sesame Street,* Batman, *The Smurfs,* and even *The Dukes of Hazzard* and *The Addams Family* inspired sets. If a show was a hit in the late 1960s and early '70s, chances are it had a Colorforms set to go along with it. And why not? They were inexpensive to produce and to purchase and a fun creative outlet for kids.

WHERE ARE THEY NOW?

The original Colorforms remain such a wonderful example of mid-twentieth-century design, they were considered for the permanent collection at the Museum of Modern Art. Reproductions of the original set are still being produced by University Games, as well as newer versions with favorite characters for today's kids. And, yes, there's a collector's market. If you have a few hundred dollars to spare, you might be able to pick up an *Addams Family* set in mint condition.

Play-Doh 1956

To baby boomers—and every generation since—there's one smell that never fails to bring back happy memories: that of fresh Play-Doh.

There are various stories about how Play-Doh was created, but all agree that it wasn't originally intended to be a toy at all, and by most accounts, it had something to do with wallpaper. As the story goes, Noah McVicker and his nephew Joe apparently were looking for a compound that could be used to clean wallpaper and only later realized their invention could be molded and played with. That's one story. Another claims Joe McVicker created the stuff out of wallpaper paste for the kids in his sister's preschool class.

WHY WE LOVED IT

However it happened, Play-Doh was an instant hit with kids, and the McVickers were quick to bring the product to market by forming the Rainbow Crafts Company. Play-Doh was originally sold in four colors—the three primary colors, plus white—first to department stores and schools in Cincinnati. Parents and teachers

loved it because it was much less messy than real clay or oil-based modeling compounds. Plus, it was reusable when stored in its airtight container.

Local toy maker Kenner soon acquired the product from Rainbow Crafts, and in 1960, Kenner

introduced the Fun Factory, a set of molds and tools that allowed kids to roll and extrude differ-

ent shapes and build other types of creations.

When Hasbro acquired Kenner, the company continued to add new colors and kits to inspire model artists.

WHERE IS IT NOW?

Today, Play-Doh is as popular as ever, and you'd be hard-pressed to find a kid, or adult for that matter, whose eyes don't light up at the sight of that bright yellow canister. In 2013, Hasbro updated the formula for the first time ever, introducing a lighter, more flexible compound.

And that smell can still trigger happy memories in legions of adults, and will surely grace the noses of many generations to come.

Crayola 64 Box of Crayons 1958

Crayola makers Binney and Smith estimate that by age six, the average child in the United States will have gone through more than seven hundred crayons. That's a lot of coloring, and crayons remain one of the staples of imagination and childhood.

Edwin Binney and C. Harold Smith founded a pigment company in 1880. In 1900, the

64
Crayola®
CRAYONS
Different Brilliant Colors
BUILT-IN SHARPENER ➡
NON-TOXIC

Crayola®
64
MORE COLORS... MORE FUN!

company introduced black wax marking pencils, and a few years later it changed schoolrooms forever in 1902 when it introduced dustless chalk. (This would prove so innovative and popular that it would win a gold medal at the St. Louis World Exposition in 1904.)

Before they would win that accolade, however, they were still trying to come up with useful items for classrooms. In working with teachers, they discovered a need for bet-

ter wax crayons and more colors. So they adapted their successful wax pencils, added different pigments, and in 1903 produced the first box of eight crayons. It sold for five cents.

It was Binney's wife, Alice, who had the final bit of inspiration and came up with the name. She took the French word for chalk, *craie,* and combined it with "oleaginous," a now obscure word meaning oily, and came up with Crayola—literally "oily chalk."

HOW DID THEY COLOR THE WORLD?

Crayola crayons were an instant hit. Over the years the company added more and more colors in bigger and bigger boxes, introducing the forty-eight-count crayon box (an unheard of number of crayons!) in 1949. But the biggest excitement, at least for the boomer generation, was yet to come. In 1958, Crayola manufactured the *sixty-four*-count box of crayons, and it became a sensation when it was introduced with much fanfare on *Captain Kangaroo*.

With this many colors, kids could be serious artists, and the new colors introduced for this box reflected an artist's palette, including Sepia, Raw Umber, and Raw Sienna, as well as the start of more trendy, fashionable colors like Plum, Lavender, and Copper. (Adding trendy colors—and retiring others—has become a standard practice for Crayola in 2013.) But what made the 64 Box really special was the built-in crayon sharpener on the back. This was *the* thing to have, and the Box became one of the bestselling toys of the year.

Crayola would continue to introduce even bigger boxes of Crayons with more crayons, but none has ever been as popular as that sixty-four-crayon box.

WHERE ARE THEY NOW?

Crayola crayons are still a top choice of moms—and coloring with them is among the most beloved memories of adults. In fact, a 2008 Yale University study ranked Crayola crayons as number eighteen on the list of the twenty most recognizable scents to American adults.

Etch A Sketch 1960

On December 24, 1960, it was a race against the clock for the Ohio Art Company, as they strove to keep their assembly line running to keep up with the phenomenal demand for its hit product—the Etch A Sketch.

Developed in France by Arthur Granjean in the late 1950s, it was originally known as L'Écran Magique (the Magic Screen), until Ohio Art brought it to the United States, gave it a new name, and turned it into an instant sensation.

In the decades since, millions have been sold in more than seventy countries worldwide. Incredibly, the basic design of the toy hasn't changed in all that time—it's a screen in a signature red frame with two knobs that control the vertical and horizontal movement of an internal stylus.

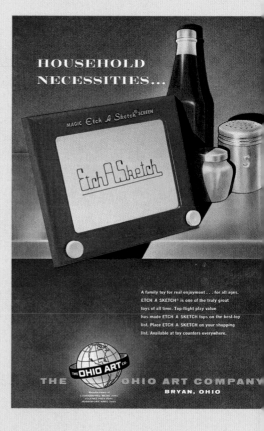

HOUSEHOLD NECESSITIES...

MAGIC Etch A Sketch® SCREEN

A family toy for real enjoyment . . . for all ages. ETCH A SKETCH® is one of the truly great toys of all time. Top-flight play value has made ETCH A SKETCH tops on the best-toy list. Place ETCH A SKETCH on your shopping list. Available at toy counters everywhere.

THE OHIO ART COMPANY
BRYAN, OHIO

HOW WE PLAYED WITH IT

But for all the millions of children who have whiled away countless hours unleashing their inner artists on their Etch A Sketch, how many actually know how the thing works? Well, the knobs control a network of strings that guide the stylus, and as it moves, it draws—or rather "etches"—into the thin film of aluminum covering the underside of the screen. When you're done, simply give the thing a shake, the aluminum powder fills in the lines, and you're ready to go again.

WHERE IS IT NOW?

In 2012, the Etch A Sketch earned unintended notoriety when presidential candidate Mitt Romney's aide Eric Fehrnstrom suggested that after the primaries, Romney's campaign could be like an Etch A Sketch. "You can kind of shake it up, and we start it all over again." Needless to say, that didn't do much for Romney's polling numbers, but it was great for Ohio Art's sales; they saw a huge boom in sales that week, and even came out with versions in red and blue to capitalize on the unexpected publicity.

DID YOU KNOW?

The Etch A Sketch was originally made by hand, and there were workers in the company's headquarters in Bryan, Ohio, who made a career of assembling the toys. It was a precise process that never changed over the years. However, in 2000, the assembly was moved to China.

Vac-U-Form 1962

The Vac-U-Form is a DIY toy that was in many ways ahead of its time. Highly sophisticated for 1962, the Vac-U-Form was a contraption that let kids design, assemble, and play with their own plastic toys. It was like having a factory in your own home, and at the time that was amazing to kids and the culture at large.

HOW WE PLAYED WITH IT

The red and silver unit had an open heating unit, a frame to hold plastic sheets, and a platform on which to place molds. To make a toy, you put a mold on the platform, put the plastic sheet in the frame, and allowed it to get soft over the heating plate. When the plastic was just the right consistency, you flipped the frame over the mold and pumped the handle on the side. The pumping created suction (hence the name "Vac-U-Form") that pulled the softened plastic around the mold (like shrink-wrap), forming half

a toy. Then you'd repeat the process to create the other half of the toy.

When the plastic had hardened, you trimmed away the excess plastic, glued the two halves together, and voilà—you had your own homemade toy. The Vac-U-Form came with a variety of molds, but as many inventive kids discovered, virtually anything small enough to fit in the unit and with a flat side that could rest on the platform could be molded. Mattel's original instruction booklet even included ideas for making your own molds from clay.

Naturally, things didn't work out perfectly every time. If the plastic wasn't soft enough, it wouldn't suction to the mold. If you left the plastic too long over the heating element, it would melt completely. But as long as you didn't ruin the piece of plastic, you could snap it back in the frame and try again. This trial-and-error process was part of the fun. Kids who played with this toy remember the joy of finding new things to mold, the

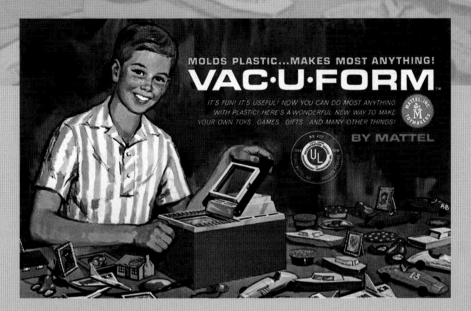

MOLDS PLASTIC...MAKES MOST ANYTHING!

VAC·U·FORM

IT'S FUN! IT'S USEFUL! NOW YOU CAN DO MOST ANYTHING WITH PLASTIC! HERE'S A WONDERFUL NEW WAY TO MAKE YOUR OWN TOYS, GAMES, GIFTS, AND MANY OTHER THINGS!

BY MATTEL

magic of watching toys take shape, and even the distinctive smell of the plastic as it heated.

Mattel ensured kids would never run out by selling refill kits—twenty-five pieces of plastic for $1.00—in all sorts of colors, including metallic gold and silver.

WHERE IS IT NOW?

The Vac-U-Form was a big hit for a year, until it was overtaken by the launch of Creepy Crawlers, which held the same DIY appeal but added the irresistible gross-out factor. In the early 1990s, Toymax tried to rein-troduce the toy as the Vac-U-Former, but it never worked as well as the original.

It's inconceivable that a toy like the Vac-U-Form would be made today. It's laughable just to think about anyone trying to sell a toy that that let kids shove lumps of plastic into an open heating unit.

Collectors still seek out the toy, but fears of fire—and litigation—have more or less sucked the Vac-U-Form into the vortex of time.

Easy-Bake Oven 1963

Other than the Barbie doll, there is probably no more iconic girls' toy of the 1960s than the Easy-Bake Oven. In fact, if you were a child of the late '60s through the late '80s you probably recall how all the girls you knew growing up automatically fell into one of two camps: those who had the Easy-Bake Oven and those who coveted it.

WHY WE LOVED IT

Debuting in 1963, with a retail price of only $15.95, the aqua-colored oven let every girl be in charge of her very own kitchen. Using four-inch pans, teeny cake mix packets, water, and the all-important lightbulb, it allowed baby boomers to have their first independent baking experiences. Their parents remember the balance of dread and pride that came with sampling the results of the efforts. The first mixes tasted pretty awful, but culinary perfection wasn't the point.

There was something about the Easy-Bake Oven that was just right for its time. Moms were poring over magazines full of easy recipes, and prepackaged foods and mixes were proliferating on store shelves. So it only made sense that girls who, at the time, foresaw a life of great food prepared with the utmost convenience, should want to mimic their moms with their very own kid-size appliance.

What worked for cakes would probably work for other types of foods, Kenner reasoned, so in 1966, the company introduced a bubble-gum-making set, but that wasn't what kids wanted to do. It was always the cakes and brownies and other concoctions that girls most loved making; they wanted to replicate what happened in a grown-up kitchen, and plus, who could resist the homey smell of a cake rising over two 100-watt bulbs?

Cooking is such an elemental role-playing activity for kids, and the Easy-Bake Oven was the first toy that truly replicated that experience. It's

never been out of production, but, of course, as kitchen styles have changed, Easy-Bake has, too. It's been made in avocado green, harvest gold, and white, as well as other colors. In fact, over the years, the Easy-Bake Oven has been restyled more than a dozen times, including one that looks like a contemporary range or a microwave.

The mixes got a lot better, too. On the oven's thirtieth anniversary in 1993, when Hasbro (which had gotten the toy in the acquisition of Kenner), surveyed grown women who were then buying the toy for the kids in their lives, the top comment was that the mixes tasted so much better than they had back in their own childhoods. To the glee of parents nationwide, they no longer had to fake delight when presented with the baking results.

WHERE IS IT NOW?

The Easy-Bake Oven is still being made in various modern models and styles today. And though their line of mixes has expanded widely to include soft and savory pretzels, s'mores, and red velvet cakes, the oven mechanism has remained largely the same.

Creepy Crawlers Thingmaker 1964

Gross has always appealed to kids. Whether the goal is to scare their sisters or prove their dominance on the playground, kids love keeping their cool while others are grossed out or scared. Few toys provide that opportunity as effectively as plastic bugs. Now imagine having a limitless supply of plastic bugs and creepy things that you could make yourself.

WHY WE LOVED IT

That was the idea behind Mattel's Creepy Crawlers set. Mattel knew from the success of its Vac-U-Form that making the toys could be as much—or more—fun than buying the toys, especially when those toys were squishy bugs—spiders, centipedes, and more. The Creepy Crawlers Thingmaker unit contained a hot plate, on which molds were placed to heat up. Plastigoop—a liquid plastic in any number of colors—was squeezed into the mold, and the toy was literally cooked. Once the bugs were baked, you attached a handle to the plate, and put it in a water bath to cool. As those who played with Creepy Crawlers might remember, the tricky part was getting the creations out of the mold;

you had to peel them out or they would rip in two.

The toy was such a hit that soon Mattel was doing a big business selling individual bottles of Plastigoop, and over the next six years, Mattel would introduce all kinds of different mold sets—famously, Creeple People and Fright Factory. For girls, flowers and gem-shaped molds soon followed.

One of the most famous extensions of the line was Incredible Edibles in 1967. Instead of plastic, this used a compound creatively named Gobble Degoop, and when heated, it formed gummy candy.

Burned fingertips were an almost inevitable hazard of playing with this toy, as eager fingers couldn't resist testing the consistency of the plastic while it was baking or trying to pull the finished product out of the mold too soon. (Remember, this was a now long-gone time when a mild burn indicated that the child hadn't used the toy correctly, not that the toy itself was flawed.)

Parents also found that the Plas-tigoop stained, and the combination of that and the open heating plate made the toy understandably less attractive over time, as parents tired of bandaging burned fingers and scrubbing plastic goop off the furniture.

WHERE IS IT NOW?

In the early 1990s, Toymax reintroduced the toy to a new generation, and it had a successful run for several years. The modern version resolved the safety issue, at least; the baking happened over a lightbulb and the molds cooked in a chamber that stayed closed until the plates were cool enough to be touched without risk.

Creepy Crawlers toys still exist, albeit in a more sanitized—and less fun—form. Rather than squirting goop into molds, kids use mechanisms to inject plastic into molds, never touching the plastic until the creation is finished. These gooey bugs will still scare or gross out your sister when strategically placed, however. It's good to know some things don't change.

Creepy Crawlers

Spirograph 1967

All toys reflect the broader culture of their times. If you were to choose a toy that was an almost perfect metaphor for 1967, it would have to be the Spirograph. The Spirograph was what happened when the space-race obsession with math and science collided headlong with the counterculture's fascination with optical art and the psychedelic. This unlikely pairing produced the Spirograph, a wonder of engineering that let kids create all kinds of trippy designs.

HOW WE PLAYED WITH IT

The toy was a simple but well-engineered collection of twenty-two plastic gears, circles, and oblongs with holes in their centers and teeth around their edges. These pieces could be interlocked in various different configurations and placed into a corrugated board where they could be held in place with small pins. Then kids put a pen through one of the holes in one of the gears and spun it around, and—voilà—instant geometric art. The pieces were designed so that even the most untalented scribbler could create intricate, cool-looking designs.

WHY WE LOVED IT

While mechanical drawing tools had been around since the late nineteenth century, Spirograph was the

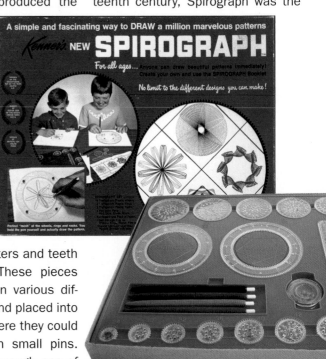

first to be marketed as a toy, and the first to tap so perfectly into the spirit of the times.

There was also something irrepressibly mod about the drawings. Even the color palette was "liberated." Kids were thrilled to find aqua, chartreuse, or even pink drawing tools on the shelves of once-boring stationery stores.

WHERE IS IT NOW?

Spirograph stuck around for several years, but, as time marched on, toy spin-art kits, and later, computer design programs made the toy less and less relevant. Finally, as the heyday of optical art passed and the culture moved on, the Spirograph spiraled into obscurity.

Over the years, several companies have tried to introduce different versions of the Spirograph, but none captivated kids like the original. In 2012, Kahootz Toys reintroduced the toy with some changes, such as replacing the drawing pins with putty. Time will tell whether it draws new fans.

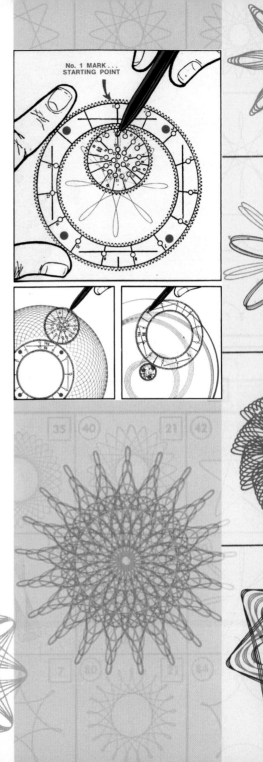

No. 1 MARK . . .
STARTING POINT

Lite-Brite 1968

I t may be hard for contemporary kids to grasp what an amazing toy Lite-Brite was, but back in 1968, a toy that could plug in and light up, letting kids create their own glowing artwork, had a serious "wow" factor.

And who could forget the jingle that got into your head like an earworm:

Lite-Brite, making things with light,
What a sight, making things with Lite-Brite.

WHY WE LOVED IT

In essence, the toy was a lightbulb in a box with holes in it. But as

LITE-BRITE
by HASBRO

CONTAINS HUNDREDS OF COLOR-GLOW PEGS IN EIGHT DIFFERENT COLORS

Create beautiful color pictures with... **LIGHT**

with all successful toys, imagination made it so much more. The set came with more than three hundred different colored pegs that could be plugged into the holes in the box to create pictures. Kids could place black construction paper pattern sheets over one side of the unit to peg by number, though plain sheets were included for those inspired to create freestyle. However, the real magic happened the moment kids switched it on, and their artwork lit up in a translucent glow.

WHERE IS IT NOW?

Though the novelty and the technology were soon overtaken by new developments, from a kid's perspective, Lite-Brite is still kind of magical, and it's become a classic. It's never been out of production. Over the years, many variations have been introduced, including a cube that let kids create on four sides. Not surprisingly, today's Lite-Brite looks more like a tablet computer and is battery operated. Lite-Brite has even inspired an app that re-creates the look of the original, though on a tiny smartphone screen. Different times bring different play, but the magic of the original Lite-Brite—at least to its first fans—will never dim.

DoodleArt 1973

Maybe it was the popularity of optical art and psychedelic posters. Maybe it was the explosion in felt-tip pens, which were still relatively new and suddenly available in the neon colors popular at the time. Whatever the source of the inspiration, in 1972, Vancouver resident Glenn Anderson came up with the idea of selling coloring to adults—or semi-adults. He created poster-size black-and-white art that you could color in yourself, and sold it with felt-tip markers. He called it DoodleArt.

The first poster was called "Ecology" and it was drawn by Len Masse. It was a true reflection of the artistic sensibility of its time with an ornate pattern of birds, flowers, and insects. Anderson packed it all in a tube and started selling it in record stores (where all the groovy adults were hanging out). The marketing slogan, also very appropriate to the times, was, "Do your own thing in color." Evidently many were eager to do just that; Anderson sold more than a million "Ecology" posters. Taking nearly sixty hours to complete, it was certainly a way to tune in and zone out . . . with or without the kind of chemical enhancements popular at the time.

WHY WE LOVED IT

DoodleArt swept Canada, the United States, and the world, a kind of underground craze that legitimized coloring for older kids and adults. New posters were produced for about five years, and many a child of the hippie generation will recall hanging their own psychedelic creations next to the lava lamps and beaded curtains in their first "grown-up" apartment or house.

WHERE IS IT NOW?

In 2011, DoodleArt changed owners, and a new era was born. Many of the original posters have been reintroduced, and coloring DoodleArt masterpieces is taking its place beside completing jigsaw puzzles as a pleasant— and once again popular—pastime.

Shrinky Dinks 1973

The Shrinky Dinks story is one of those that inspire people to try to get into the toy business. As the tale goes, a suburban mom named Betty Morris was looking for an activity to do with her Boy Scout troop and came across an article in a crafts magazine that said you could make Christmas ornaments out of clear plastic coffee can lids; just decorate the lid and bake it over low heat and the plastic would magically shrink. She tried it, and it worked.

While many people would simply be grateful that this experiment didn't burn the house down, Betty and her friend Kathryn Bloomberg turned it into a huge business.

It was such a simple product that they were able to make it themselves, and the first season of sales put them—and their little town of Brookfield, Wisconsin—on the map.

WHY WE LOVED THEM

Kids would draw on or color the sheets (through trial and error, Morris and Bloomberg managed to find a type of plastic sheeting that melted just like the coffee lids), place them in a conventional or toaster oven, and watch them shrink to a fraction of their original size while they also thickened and grew more durable. More fun still, with a windowed oven, kids could actually *watch* their pieces shrink. This bonus was a big part of what turned an otherwise basic arts and crafts project into a huge hit toy.

WHERE ARE THEY NOW?

In 2001, Spin Master introduced an oven play set called the Incredible Shrinky Dinks Maker, and it was one of the hottest toys of the year—certainly a distinction not often given to an arts and crafts kit. Today, there are many different companies making shrinking plastic, but the original Shrinky Dinks are now made by Big Time toys.

The excitement, though, as any kid who played with them will remember, was that when their Shrinky Dinks creations were baked, it didn't *feel* like arts and crafts; it felt like magic.

DID YOU KNOW?

Here's how it works: Soft polystyrene plastic is put through rollers to create thin sheets. When low heat is applied to the sheet, the polymer reacts by returning partially to its original form. The material then becomes thicker and shrinks to approximately one-third of its original size.

Fashion Plates **1978**

The 1970s marked the beginning of the era of the fashion designer as celebrity: From Ralph Lauren to Calvin Klein to Yves Saint Laurent to Laura Ashley and many more, high-end designers suddenly were in the public eye just as often—if not more often—as their models.

So it's no surprise that kids would want to pretend to be fashion designers. This is why, in 1978, the toy maker Tomy introduced Fashion Plates, a set of plastic plates with raised outlines of different fashion pieces: hats, shirts, skirts, and so on. Kids would choose their outlines, assemble the plates, lay a piece of paper over the top, and then, with a pencil or marker, rub the paper to create an outline of the full outfit. Then the real fun began: coloring and decorating the outfit any way they chose.

WHY WE LOVED IT

Like so many arts and crafts toys from the 1960s on, the idea was to allow kids who might not be gifted artists to create a professional-looking result.

The toy is also a wonderful snapshot of mainstream fashion of the late 1970s; in the original you'll find peasant blouses, maxi skirts, and bell-bottoms, to name a few.

WHERE ARE THEY NOW?

As those of us who remember our '70s bell-bottoms with various degrees of embarrassment know well,

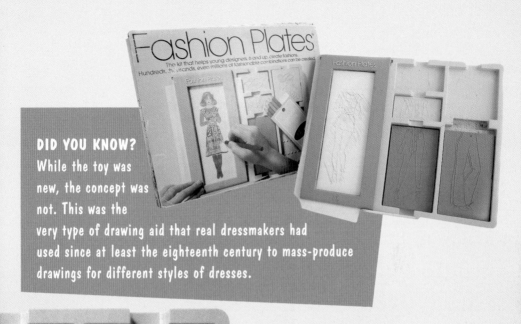

fashion eventually marches on. The original plates quickly became dated as fashions changed dramatically in the early 1980s, and Tomy got out of the business. Other companies started to produce similar but more up-to-date products, and rubbing art is still common in a variety of arts and crafts toys.

Having already lasted for a couple of centuries, it is not likely that this type of toy will ever disappear entirely, even now that computers can so easily replicate drawings. The fun of drawing and designing is timeless, even if fashion is not, and you'll find some version of this type of toy for sale every year.

Snoopy Sno-Cone Machine 1979

I f you were a kid in 1979, you may remember how the Snoopy Sno-Cone Machine first won your heart with its now-classic commercial. Who could forget those ever-cheerful girls who chirped "It's yummy, Snoopy"? And those girls made it look so easy.

WHY WE LOVED IT

As with many kitchen play sets, the fun was more in the making than the eating. The plastic unit was shaped like Snoopy's dog house— complete with Snoopy, as per usual, on the roof. Kids dropped cubes of ice into the top and turned the crank on the back, and shavings fell into a cup, using the Snoopy figure on top of a plunger to push the ice into the grinder. The ice could be flavored with Kool-Aid, syrup, or any other kind of sugary goodness.

As impressive as the sno-cone machine looked in the TV commercials, it wasn't the most functional appliance. It took lots of ice to even partially fill the cup, and the ice shavings had a tendency to melt before a convincing sno-cone could be made. None of that mattered to kids, however; as the fun was in the shredding, not getting a professional or even edible result.

WHERE IS IT NOW?

Once the commercial was taken off the air, the toy faded, though every few years different companies would try to revive it, trading mostly on the nostalgia factor and targeting those Gen Xers who had wanted a Snoopy Sno Cone Machine and not gotten it, and were keen to rectify that terrible injustice by buying one for their own kids.

In 2012, Cra-Z-Art launched an almost exact replica of the original, down to the fact that it was better at making a delicious slushy mess than recognizable sno-cones.

SNOOPY

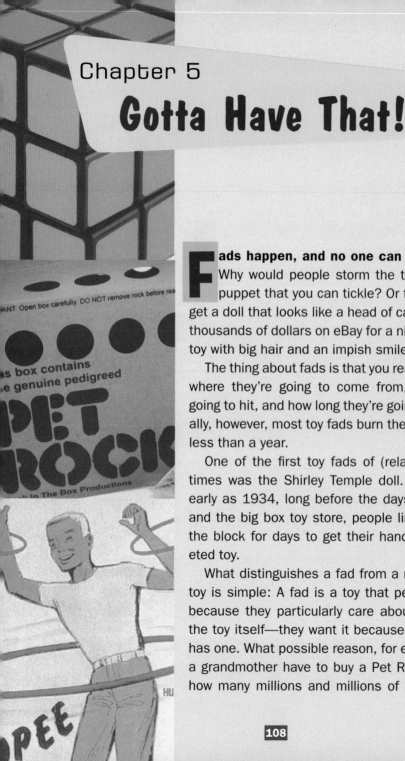

Chapter 5

Gotta Have That!

Fads happen, and no one can predict them. Why would people storm the toy aisles for a puppet that you can tickle? Or fly to Europe to get a doll that looks like a head of cabbage? Or bid thousands of dollars on eBay for a nine-inch plastic toy with big hair and an impish smile?

The thing about fads is that you really never know where they're going to come from, when they're going to hit, and how long they're going to last. Usually, however, most toy fads burn themselves out in less than a year.

One of the first toy fads of (relatively) modern times was the Shirley Temple doll. Even back as early as 1934, long before the days of the TV ad and the big box toy store, people lined up around the block for days to get their hands on this coveted toy.

What distinguishes a fad from a merely popular toy is simple: A fad is a toy that people want not because they particularly care about or even like the toy itself—they want it because everyone else has one. What possible reason, for example, would a grandmother have to buy a Pet Rock? Similarly, how many millions and millions of people bought

Rubik's Cubes knowing full well there was maybe one chance in a million they'd actually be able to figure the darn thing out? Fads have always been more about fitting in and seeming "cool" than about the actual toys.

Fads, however, are significant in what they say about our culture. It's no coincidence, for example, that the hula hoop took hold at a time when Americans were beginning to cast off the moral strictures of the Eisenhower years. Moreover, fads provide a unifying cultural experience that mark certain moments in time. After all, if you were alive and conscious, don't you remember when riots broke out in toy store aisles over the Tickle Me Elmo doll? Or when everyone was clamoring to get their hands on a Pet Rock? It just goes to show that no matter how silly and idiotic the toy, once something becomes a fad, kids everywhere *have* to have one—at least until the fad flames out, and then it's amazing how quickly kids move on.

In the years after the runaway success of the Cabbage Patch Kids, toy makers everywhere became obsessed with creating the next big fad. Yet real fads can't be created by any level of marketing or promotion; they have to happen organically—and very often they make absolutely no sense. But that's a big part of the fun.

Hula Hoops 1958

Once a toy fad starts spinning, it takes on a life of its own. That's exactly what happened when the hula hoop hit the United States in July 1958. By the time the craze reached its height about four months later, more than twenty-five million hula hoops had already been sold.

Marketed as a gravity-defying toy that could rotate "perpetually with body-english," the hula hoop was the first fad to completely sweep the nation, transcending barriers of geography, class, race, and even age. Sure, there had been hugely popular toys before (people had stood in long lines for the Shirley Temple doll, for example) but this was the first post–World War II toy that seemed to take the entire culture by storm. And if people weren't hula hooping, they

WHAM-O

ORIGINAL

hula-hoop

AMAZING
DEFIES GRAVITY

were talking about it. Hula hoops were everywhere: on TV, in the movies, and even on the society pages as stars such as Jane Russell at the opening of a new nightclub tried their hands—and hips—at it.

The guys behind the hula hoop were Arthur "Spud" Melin and Richard Knerr, founders of Wham-O (maker of the Frisbee). Interestingly, their inspiration for the toy that soon became as American as apple pie actually came from faraway Australia, where they had seen children playing with bamboo hoops in a gym class. It looked like fun, so the partners decided to make hoops out of plastic and sell them as toys. They called them hula hoops because the gyrations of the hips required to keep the hoops up looked a lot like the Hawaiian dance, or so they thought.

However, the hula hoop wasn't an instant hit. So, Melin and Knerr, guerilla marketers ahead of their time, hit the streets of Southern California, giving away hundreds of hoops to kids at playgrounds and on the beaches. Like virtually every fad (and virtually every hula hoop), once set in motion, it's easy to forget how hard it was to get off the ground.

WHY WE LOVED THEM

The hula hoop is an archetypal toy fad, made possible by the convergence of several cultural events. The first was the rise of youth culture and the growing influence of national media, whose portrayal of the hoop in television, magazines, and newspapers quickly made hula hooping synonymous with everything young and energetic. (When has such marketing ever failed?) Plus, teenage baby boomers were starting to rebel against the strict formality of the Eisenhower years. Rock and roll was already getting this new generation to swing their hips, so why not try to keep a plastic hoop revolving around your midsection—or other body parts?

And it wasn't just "those crazy kids" who loved them. Adults were swept along with the hip new craze as well. Wham-O quickly realized this and began to make them in larger sizes that would be easier for adults to use.

WHERE ARE THEY NOW?

Like every hot-burning craze, the hula hoop eventually cooled down, but the classic toy has never been without a loyal fan base and has never been off the market. In 1967, Wham-O caused a minicraze with

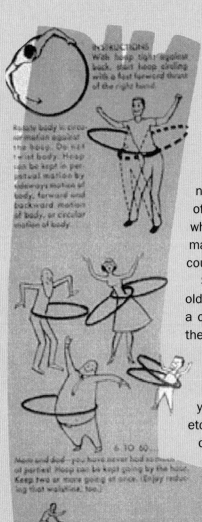

the Shoop Shoop Hula Hoop, simply a hula hoop with quarter-inch ball bearings inside the ring so that when it swung around, it made a "shoop shoop" sound. Like with many toys of that era, a catchy TV commercial made it a must-have for a time.

Over the years, many other companies jumped into the ring with all kinds of frills, such as Maui Toys' Wave Hoop, whose liquid core, the company claimed, made it "ten times easier to spin." (You couldn't prove that by me.)

Still, there is no substitute for the plain old original hula hoop. Whether you were a child of the 1960s, '70s, '80s, or even the '90s, you surely have a memory of that very first time you tried to hula hoop, only to have it fall right to your ankles (it looked so easy!), etched in your mind. The hula hoop will be similarly etched into American history books as one of the greatest fads of all time.

Trolls 1959

I f you're a child of the 1980s it may surprise you to learn that Trolls have actually been delighting children and collectors for more than half a century. Danish craftsman Thomas Dam created the homely, impish-looking creatures in 1959, but it would be several more years before they became popular in the United States. In fact, it was one of the first toy fads in history to transcend gender lines, a phenomenon that wouldn't be seen on such a scale again until the Beanie Babies craze of the 1990s. And Trolls weren't just for kids. Trolls were everywhere: Celebrities, rock stars, and even the First Lady were photographed with these strange-looking, but oddly irresistible, dolls.

WHY WE LOVED THEM

As the legend goes, Trolls were mystical creatures who lived in the woods, granted wishes, and lived for carefree good times for all. No wonder they were popular with the emerging youth culture of the early 1960s!

Plus, for Trolls, it was always a bad hair day, and that was part of their appeal. Their wrinkled faces, big ears, and silly, impish grins made them seem mysterious (what were they up to, anyway?) and unlike any other doll on the market.

WHERE ARE THEY NOW?

After the Trolls' first flush of popularity, the craze—like every fad—ran its course, and by 1966, kids had turned to new things. But you can't keep a good Troll down, and in 1987, Russ Berrie, who had been known for his plush teddy bears and children's gifts, built a whole new business reintroducing the Trolls to consumers. As with many second-wave toy fads, this generation of Trolls was more diverse than the first; there were Rasta Trolls and priest Trolls and wizard Trolls and Trolls with hair in all colors of the rainbow. And, in turn, a whole new generation of Troll lovers (perhaps seeking a respite from the saccharine cuteness of the Care Bears and Strawberry Shortcake) had to have them all, making Trolls one of the most popular collectibles (second only to Barbie) in recent toy history.

DID YOU KNOW? Maybe it was their crazy hair, or their mischievous grins, but for whatever reason, Trolls were hot in Hollywood, making memorable cameos on a number of popular TV shows and movies of the early 1990s. Synclaire James-Jones (Kim Coles), Queen Latifah's amiable receptionist on the '90s Fox sitcom *Living Single*, was an avid collector of Trolls, and Trolls have also shown up on episodes of *Step by Step*, *Friends*, *The Simpsons*, and other sitcoms. More recently, they inspired the look for the character of Rumpelstiltskin in *Shrek Forever After*, and made an appearance in the opening sequence of *Toy Story 3*.

Wizzzer 1969

There are few toys older than spinning tops. Tops have been found buried in the Pyramids, presumably stored for play in the next world. And virtually every culture since has had some kind of top. So after a few millennia, there's probably not much one could do to reinvent this basic, right?

Wrong. In 1969, Mattel added a gyroscope to the inner workings of the top, eliminated the string, and created a winding mechanism with a rubber tip that players could rev up on a hard surface, so all it took was a tiny bit of effort to get the top spinning.

WHY WE LOVED THEM

Thanks to the gyroscope, the spinning tops could do all kinds of tricks, and this is what made Wizzzers such a hit. Wizzzers could balance on the tip of a pencil, dance along a string, even spin perpendicularly to the floor. Kids quickly created their own tricks and games with them, including battling with other Wizzzers, of course.

They became a hot collectible, and Mattel swiftly rolled out different colors and styles. Most of them were two-toned with one color on

top and one on the bottom, and they had two different shapes—one round and one more squared off. This was primarily because it looked cool when they spun.

The fun didn't come without a cost. More than a few tables' finishes were bruised as casualties of play, and ground rules for damage-free Wizzzers play were instituted in many homes.

WHERE ARE THEY NOW?

Like most fads, Wizzzers spun out after a couple of years. They were brought back briefly by Playtime Toys as a reproduction of the originals, but the craze had passed, and kids, as they do, had moved on.

However, tops are one of the oldest playthings known to humans, so it was inevitable that top play would make a comeback. In 2002, Hasbro launched a line of battling tops called Beyblade, and they created a sensation, spawning a TV show and much more. Duncan (the yo-yo people) soon put their own spin on the classic toy by rolling out Wiz-z-zers, tops reinvented as robotic battlers.

In 2013, Mattel went back to their top-flight inspiration with the introduction of Hot Wheels Spin Shotz, tops that spin, battle, do stunts, and run along a track—proof positive that millennia from now kids will probably still find something stimulating in playing with tops.

Clackers c.1970

Also known as Klik Klaks (among many other variations), Clackers were one of those toys originally developed as a weapon (along with yo-yos and boomerangs). Its original use was to knock out small animals while hunting.

HOW WE PLAYED WITH THEM

The toy was nothing more than two colored acrylic balls at either end of a piece of string, and play involved holding the string at its center and moving one's hand up and down to make the balls smack together, which made a sharp noise (hence the name). Good players could get the balls going fast enough so they hit each other above and below the hand—it was all in the centripetal force.

There was quite a learning curve involved, and repeated practice resulted in many a banged hand. Like yo-yos and other simple, inexpensive toys that could fit into a pants pocket, Clackers inspired schoolyard competitions, and proficiency conferred great status on the adept.

This was also a toy that inspired urban legends. Many kids of the 1970s knew a kid who knew a kid at a school across town who had gotten glass Clackers and been seriously injured—or *nearly died*—doing some outrageous feat with the toy. Most of these stories were complete fabrications, of course, but they added an irresistible whiff of danger to the play—always appealing in the schoolyard.

WHERE ARE THEY NOW?

As Clackers became more and more popular with kids, they became equally *un*popular with educators. As the tall tales of gory Clackers injuries began to trickle up to teachers and administrators, many schools banned them, and without the ability to show off at recess, kids soon lost interest.

It's hard to imagine that in today's world any company would try to reintroduce these—the threat of lawsuits would be enough to scare any manufacturer away. Attempts to produce the toy with safer plastic balls never caught on, largely because they didn't work very well, and, more important, they didn't "clack."

For today's safety-conscious

parents, many of whom may have played with these as kids, Clackers have been permanently filed under "What were we thinking?" For the ardent fan, however, who wants to revisit those glory days—and bruised hands—there are still some places that sell them. If you go there, you're on your own.

Pet Rock 1975

Was the Pet Rock a toy? Well, maybe it was more of a joke. The rock came in a box with air holes and a tongue-in-cheek manual about how to care for and train your new pet. It talked about different "breeds" of pet rocks, explained how to teach your Pet Rock to attack (throw it), and offered various tips for domesticating your pet—a razor sharp parody of traditional pet-training books.

This made headlines in the silly season for news, and people found it so hilarious, they went out in droves and bought pet rocks as jokes and gifts.

WHERE IS IT NOW?

Not surprisingly, the fad passed quite quickly. (After all, once the joke had been made, why would anyone have any use for a Pet Rock?) Within six months Pet Rocks had all but disappeared, but not before earning Dahl, and toy store owners everywhere, a quick pile of money.

Today, the Pet Rock is nothing more than a memory, though in honor of its silly place in our cultural history, the company Basic Fun created a collectible key ring, as they did for many kitschy products.

The originals, I'm guessing, have largely continued the process of returning to the soil. We'll check back in a geological age . . . or two.

DID YOU KNOW?
As the legend goes, California advertising executive Gary Dahl conceived of the idea after hearing his friends talk about how difficult it was to take care of their pets.

k before reading instructions

INSTRUCTION BOOK

THE PET ROCK

Rubik's Cube 1980

I n the early 1980s, there were few greater presumed indicators of intelligence than the speed with which one could solve a Rubik's Cube. Solving it in under an hour was respectable. Fifteen minutes was impressive. Five minutes or less? A mark of genius (not to mention a great party trick). And those who failed again and again to line up all six colors on all six sides of the cube? Well, they just weren't that smart, were they?

The 3 x 3 x 3-inch cube with nine colored squares on each side was created by Hungarian Erno Rubik in 1974, but it would be another six years before the fad truly became a global phenomenon, with virtually everyone on the planet eager to give it a try—brainiac or no.

The cube might have stayed behind the Iron Curtain indefinitely had it not been for Dr. Tibor Laczi, who "discovered" it on a trip to Budapest. Captivated, he took it to the Nuremberg, Germany, Toy Fair in January 1979 but initially found no distributors interested in taking a chance on a little puzzle. That is, until he met Tom Kremer, a toy inventor who brought the cube to the United States and sold the rights to Ideal.

By this time, the cube phenomenon was spreading across the globe, a veritable pandemic in plastic. In 1980, the year the cube was unveiled in the United States, more than a million units were sold, and this number grew exponentially each successive year.

But this astonishing level of success almost backfired, as counterfeit cubes soon started cropping up everywhere. Although the name was protected, the mechanism that made it all work was easy enough to copy, so many companies all over the world started to introduce knock-offs under such creative names as "magic cube" "magic square," and "magic box." Ultimately, the market flooded, and at Ideal's warehouse in the Hollis neighborhood of Queens, cartons of unsold or returned cubes were stacked as far as the eye could see.

But Kremer wasn't going to give up. He bought back the rights to the cube and in 1995, the toy company OddzOn Products relaunched it with a whole line of Rubik's branded puzzles, including a pyramid-shaped Rubik's Cube, a Sudoku Rubik's Cube, and the Pentamix, billed as the world's hardest Rubik's Cube. This brought the toy back into the public eye, and people started to play with it again.

WHY WE LOVED IT

The Rubik's Cube was groundbreaking for being the first puzzle that stayed in one piece *while* it was being solved.

In fact, the interior mechanism of the Rubik's Cube (Go ahead. Look inside. You've always wanted an excuse to whack it with a hammer anyway.) is one of the engineering marvels of

twentieth-century toy design.

Each cube in the center of the six sides is secured to an internal mechanism. They actually never move. The cubes on either side of the center cube on the same line can move up or down. The cubes on the corners can move both up and down *and* left and right. So, the trick is to know which cubes can move where and how to get them all lined up. Don't let the fact that there are forty-three quintillion (that's a one with eighteen zeros) possible combinations on the original 3 x 3 x 3 cube slow you down, sport.

WHERE IS IT NOW?

The Rubik's Cube has been front-page news and a prop on countless TV shows and movies. There have been nearly seventy books written on the cube, including dozens of handbooks on how to solve it. It graces the pages of nearly every major dictionary and it even became a Saturday morning superhero in *Rubik, the Amazing Cube.*

POGs 1991

Aside, perhaps, from the most diehard fans, few today recall that POG is an acronym for Passion Fruit Orange Guava, a drink sold by the Haleakala Dairy on the island of Maui. In fact, POG caps originated as the cardboard discs that the dairy used to seal the glass juice bottles.

HOW WE PLAYED WITH THEM

For years these were a novelty among Hawaiian kids, who not only collected the caps but invented a basic game in which players tried to flip over as many caps as possible by hitting a stack of the caps with a larger disc or "slammer." Those that flipped over became the property of the person who threw the slammer, and the goal, naturally, was to amass as many as possible. It was the kind of game every kid on the block could play since so many of them drank the juice; plus, refreshing the toy supply was easy and inexpensive.

That might have been the end of it, but the game caught on, and soon kids all over Maui were playing the game. Once the Canadian company Stanpac, which had made the bottle caps for the Haleakala Dairy, caught on to the fact that the game was all the rage across Maui, they started printing and shipping the caps as game pieces. It wasn't long before California entrepreneur Alan Rypinski bought the trademark from the dairy and started the World POG Federation.

WHY WE LOVED THEM

By 1993, the game had spread throughout the United States, and virtually every company with a logo or a marketing department was printing POGs, which only fueled the collecting mania among kids. It was the perfect storm of toy capitalism. The caps were cheap to produce and give away, and how often do kids clamor to be advertised to? POGs were used to promote everything from toy lines to movies to sports teams and even antidrug campaigns.

As with everything that's popular in the schoolyard, controversy soon followed. Some schools banned

POGs because kids were playing "for keeps," which school officials considered akin to gambling. (It *was* gambling.) At the same time, avid collectors wouldn't think of playing with POGs in the schoolyard, lest their precious collectibles get messed up in play.

WHERE ARE THEY NOW?

As often happens with fads, POGs burned hot and fast. It took nearly two years for POGs to make their trek eastward from Hawaii and become a nationwide sensation, but once the market was saturated with them, kids moved on . . . as kids usually do. By 1994, aside from a few pockets of activity, POGs had had their day in the spotlight.

In 2006, Funrise tried to reintroduce POGs, thinking that a new generation of kids would love them just as much as their '90s forebears. They were called Slammer Whammers, and they had a fairly modest success, but just as you can't predict a fad, you can't repeat one, and Funrise got out of the business within a year.

Chapter 6

Boys Will Be Boys

When you're a little boy, and your life is all about "Eat your peas," "Do your homework," "Get in the car," and so forth, you don't feel very powerful. Let's face it, when your life is controlled by "the evil grown-ups," superpowers would sure come in handy. OK, so maybe I'm oversimplifying and/or overdramatizing, but there is no denying the fact that traditional play for boys has always been about finding power and strength through fantasy, whether it's taking on the persona of a superhero, being at the helm of a powerful machine, or battling the evil forces to keep them from ruling the world.

Of course, there are and have always been girls who enjoy this kind of play, too; it's not necessarily restricted to gender. However, whether it's nature or nurture (and I'm not here to debate that point), in general, action-based play appeals more to boys, just as doll play tends to appeal to girls. In the late 1990s, my company constructed a play test where we put boys and girls in a room with traditional boys' and girls' toys. Within a few minutes, we observed the boys reaching for the Hot Wheels cars and Tonka trucks, while the girls waged an all-out Barbie battle. While this certainly wasn't scientific research, it did show that these particular kids were drawn to the toys typically associated with their gender.

The fact is, most boys gravitate toward play that involves power and dominance. (And "most" is what drives the mass-market toy business.) In the years after World War II, as the nation was adjusting to peacetime, growing prosperity, and a booming infrastructure, classic building toys such as trucks and Erector sets were the most popular boys' toys. The culture was definitely pushing boys into standardized male roles, and toys reflected that.

However, everything changed with the launch of G.I. Joe, the first so-called action figure—an acceptable euphemism for "doll for boys." The post-WWII years were a patriotic time when few things were more macho than being a soldier, and by the mid-1960s G.I. Joe had become the ultimate role model—and the most popular toy—among legions of red-blooded American boys. Because play always reflects the larger culture, as the Cold War pressed on, military play gave way to spy-based play, and military reenactment with pretend armaments such as Johnny Seven O.M.A. took center stage. Then, in the later years of the Vietnam conflict, the military went out of style entirely and action figures—including Major Matt Mason and the *Star Wars* characters—took to space. When the space race ended and the relatively peaceful 1980s rolled around, young boys found villains to battle in the realm of future and fantasy with toys such as He-Man and the Masters of the Universe and the Transformers.

Yet whatever superpowers they had and whoever their enemies were, the one thing all these toys had in common was that they allowed boys to let their imaginations run wild and act out their heroic fantasies. Whether those fantasies involved space exploration, defending the universe against invaders, or ambushing their little sisters with an Air Blaster, the play was all about creating a world where *they* were in control—one where mom couldn't force them to finish their math homework or eat their peas.

Tonka Trucks 1947

As the United States emerged from World War II and construction boomed around the country, it was only natural that kids would clamor for toy versions of all the cranes and steam shovels and construction trucks they saw all around them.

Mound Metalcraft was founded in a schoolhouse basement in Mound, Minnesota, near Lake Minnetonka—the body of water that would ultimately inspire the company's re-branded name. Originally founded to produce metal garden supplies, Mound Metalcraft started making a line of toy vehicles to keep the lights on during the gardening off season.

WHY WE LOVED THEM

In 1947, the company produced about thirty-seven thousand individual trucks in two styles: a crane and a steam shovel. These were some tough toys, and they stood up to hard-playing kids. They became such hits that Mound Metalcraft ultimately abandoned gardening, changed its name to Tonka, and, quite literally, beat its plowshares into an ever-growing fleet of toy vehicles.

Boys and girls alike loved Tonka trucks for the realism of the play and the fact that they were virtually indestructible. Sure, the trucks could rust, but a little naval jelly and a paint job, and they were good as new all over again.

In 1965, Tonka introduced what would become its bestselling truck ever—the Tonka Mighty Dump Truck.

Eventually Tonka started making the trucks out of plastic, or partially out of plastic, but they were still the strongest toys out there, and kids still loved them.

WHERE ARE THEY NOW?

Tonka trucks are still an integral and memorable part of many childhoods (and for girls, too!). After years of being made out of plastic, in 2012, some of the classics have been reintroduced and made of steel as they were originally. It seems that it's not just the trucks themselves, but the fun of creating a mini construction site in the sandbox that remains indestructible.

Even as the trucks acquired lights, sounds, electronics, and characters, no individual Tonka truck would ever outsell this one—especially once Tonka produced the now-classic commercial of an elephant unable to crush the indomitable truck.

Matchbox Cars

For almost as long as there have been real cars, there have been toy cars. After all, few innovations have captured the imagination of kids and adults alike as much as the automobile. Some of the earliest toy cars, dating back to the 1920s, were large replicas made of sheet metal. Then, in the 1930s, German model makers began to produce smaller die-cast (molded metal) toy cars.

But how the Matchbox cars came about is one of those happy accidents of the toy business. Leslie Smith and Rodney Smith (unrelated) had been lifelong friends, living in London. In the years after World War II, as London began to build itself back up from its near destruction, Leslie and Rodney saw a demand for all kinds of small die-cast metal. So they joined forces with a designer named Jack Odell and built a successful manufacturing business. As London recovered and demand for their products dropped, the partners realized they could offset their slow business period by making toys and toy parts.

It was Odell who, in 1952, discovered the market for miniaturized toy vehicles. His daughter had just started school and, like all kids, she wanted to take some toys along with her. The school, however, allowed children to only carry toys that fit in a matchbox. So Odell made a

model of a small road roller, put it into a matchbox, and sent her off to school. Pretty soon, all the kids wanted one, too, and a new toy was born. (The name was a no-brainer.)

WHY WE LOVED THEM

In the first year, four toys were produced under the Matchbox name, marketed as a "toy that is a complete toy" for under a dollar. Shortly thereafter, Matchbox Series 1–75 was born.

The cars' popularity quickly spread throughout England to the United States, and all over the world. In 1956, the company expanded the line and introduced the Models of Yesteryear—a collection of classics that appealed to an ever-growing number of fans.

WHERE ARE THEY NOW?

Matchbox cars are still being made, and while the antique replicas are no longer part of the line, those models live on through many active collectors and collector's groups and conventions. Even as the brand has matured, what has never been lost is the endless fascination and imagination that children of all ages bring to a car that is small enough to fit inside a matchbox.

Johnny Reb Cannon 1961

More than half a century later, it may be difficult to remember the craze that the 1957–65 Civil War Centennial caused. Civil War mania swept the nation, as the post office issued Civil War stamps, the National Parks Service restored Civil War battlefields, and history enthusiasts nationwide staged Civil War reenactments with a level of detail and accuracy that would have surely made their high school history teachers beam with pride.

The toy business, as usual, seized the opportunity, and that's where Remco's Johnny Reb Cannon, a plastic replica of a Civil War–era cannon, came into the picture. It sat on a caisson and flew the Confederate flag, and even came with four hollow cannonballs with a hole through the center of each. Kids simply threaded a ball onto a rod in the cannon and used the ramrod (included) to push the ball all the way down, cocking the firing mechanism. With a pull on the string, the ball would shoot as far as thirty-five feet.

WHY WE LOVED IT

The toy was hugely popular, even though there wasn't a lot of power in it. What young boy wouldn't want a toy that could shoot cannonballs at unsuspecting moms, sister, and playground rivals?

WHERE IS IT NOW?

The toy sold for a couple of years but disappeared—along with most of the Civil War mania—after the centennial celebrations ended.

In 2006, *Radar* magazine named the Johnny Reb Cannon one of the Ten Most Dangerous Toys of All Time. True, the balls stung if they hit you, but any kid with the slightest bit of common sense knew to get out of the way—or get his revenge when it was his turn to fire.

Outside the odd posting on an auction site, the Johnny Reb Cannon is virtually impossible to find. Given current sensibilities, it's unlikely that any toys celebrating the Civil War will ever make a comeback.

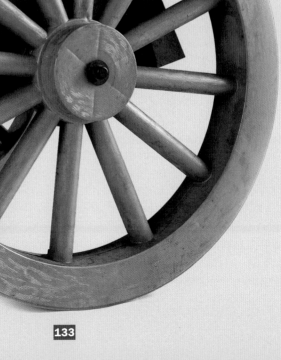

Air Blaster 1963

The commercial claimed it could "blow out candles at 20-feet." So, clearly kids everywhere had to try it. And it worked. The Wham-O Air Blaster looked like it was straight out of outer space—or at least the popular conceptions of what outer space might look like. To get the air blasting, you cocked the lever on the top, and a bladder inside was stretched back and locked in place. When you pulled the trigger, the bladder released, pushing the air in the large-ish chamber through a narrow opening at the front of the barrel, and shooting out air in one large—and loud—burst.

HOW WE PLAYED WITH IT

Included with the Air Blaster was a hanging target—a picture of a gorilla that, when hit with the blast of air, would wave in the resulting breeze. The game was to see how far away you could make the target move.

Kids being kids, much of the fun was also in sneaking up behind people and shooting them with a blast of air, which inevitably resulted in arguments, confiscation, and being sent to one's room, but was worth it.

The hugely popular toy spawned some urban legends, such as the kid who had his eardrums shot out by a blast of air. This never happened, of course, but it made for a good story, particularly when menacing smaller siblings with a cocked Air Blaster.

WHERE IS IT NOW?

The Air Blaster stuck around for only a couple of years, which was pretty common for novelty toys at that time. As cool as it was, the toy had limited play. Once you'd blown out a candle and popped the target a few times, scared the cat or made your brothers jump, that was pretty much it. Plus, despite the fact that no injuries were reported, parents weren't so keen on it, perhaps because the repeated loud pops were more annoying than dangerous.

Today the toy is rare, even on auction sites. Over the years, the inside chamber would decompose, so it's even rarer to find one that works. Half a century later, it's now just a blast from the past.

AIR BLASTER

THE MOST AMAZING TOY EVER INVENTED!
Shoot FREE AMMO all day long!

SHOOTS A TERRIFIC AIR BLAST 40 FEET!

INVISIBLE
AIR BLASTER
with action TARGET

ANT GORILLA DISINTEGRATES
HEN HIT...THEN SNAPS BACK!

No. 249 INDIVIDUALLY PACKED IN
COLORFUL DISPLAY BOX.
PACKED 6 TO A CARTON
SHIPPING WT. 16½ LBS.

G.I. Joe 1964

The vast majority of boys and men alive today have never lived in a world without action figures. But the action figure is only about fifty years old. Sure, there were those crudely molded tiny little green army men, and in the 1920s and '30s there were even little toy soldiers made of—gasp—lead, but fifty years ago, anything on the scale of our modern-day action figures, complete with personalities and highly developed backstories, would have been considered dolls for boys, and that would never do.

That all changed in 1962, when Don Levine, creative director for Hasbro, was approached about creating children's toys for an upcoming TV series called *The Lieutenant*. Levine passed on the opportunity because he thought the show wasn't for kids, but the idea for a character based on the military wouldn't quite get out of his head.

Yet, as Vincent Santelmo describes in *The Complete Encyclopedia of G.I. Joe,* it was actually an artist's mannequin that finally inspired Levine to create a plaything based on young boys' military heroes. Since the play

G.I. JOE
ACTION SOLDIER T.M.
by HASBRO®

America's *movable* fighting man

·MOVE 'G.I. 'JOE' INTO
ACTION POSITIONS

would have to be all about action, the twelve-inch figure would have twenty-one movable parts to be able to act out any make-believe combat situation.

In Levine's mind, this would make Joe much more than a doll, but the doll problem lingered, and initial response to the concept from the toy industry was lukewarm (as was the initial reaction to Barbie, by the way). Still, Hasbro had already invested two years and more than $2 million in the toy solider concept, so Levine—and Joe—got the green light.

Lucky for them, it turned out that kids wanted Joe—to the tune of $18 million in the first year alone. Even-

America's *movable* fighting man ™

·MOVE 'G.I. 'JO

1964–1994 G.I. JOE
"A REAL AMERICAN HERO"

tually two out of three boys in the United States would have a G.I. Joe, and at one time the line represented 70 percent of Hasbro's business.

WHY WE LOVED HIM

In the mid-1960s, soldiers were everywhere, especially on television—from the serious series such as *Combat!* to the comedies of *Hogan's Heroes* and *Gomer Pyle USMC*. In the years after the Korean War and while there was still support for the Vietnam conflict, there was no bigger hero than a solider and, thus, no more attractive a role model—and thus a toy—for young boys.

Yet the escalating conflict in Vietnam would have a profound impact on G.I. Joe. When Operation Rolling Thunder, the first sustained American assault on North Vietnam, began in 1965, the military was still seen as heroic. However, as the political landscape changed and support for the war dwindled, G.I. Joe had to respond, or be left behind. So in the 1970s, he loosened his ties with the military and became, simply, a more generic hero. He was an adventurer on land, sea, and air rather than a military figure. Yet he was still a hero who also went to space and, for a time, had lifelike hair. And who can forget G.I. Joe with Kung Fu Grip? It's still a punch line for adults. His story lines became more and more abstract as Joe found new nemeses *off* the battlefield. In the Reagan years, for example, Joe had new adventures on a popular TV show, going to space, tracking mummies, and battling enemies far removed from the real world of combat. It was a long way from his early days in the classic arenas of the army, air force, navy, and marines.

WHERE IS HE NOW?

All tours of duty eventually end, but not this one. The G.I. Joe collector community is large and loyal, and he's been featured in one major motion picture and in another in 2013. In this case the old soldier didn't fade away at all; he became an entertainment franchise. In the minds of young boys who grew up in the 1960s and beyond, Joe will always be a Real American Hero, if not only for his heroic actions on the battlefield, then for creating a whole new way for boys to play with—yes—dolls.

Johnny Seven O.M.A. 1964

For boys who liked combat play, few toys are as fondly remembered as the Johnny Seven O.M.A. (One Man Army) from Topper Toys.

In the mid-1960s, the idea of the lone action hero, while not exactly new, was experiencing a revival. Still a few years before Vietnam War opposition would reach its peak, this was a time when soldiers were still seen as real-life heroes.

WHY WE LOVED IT

The Johnny Seven O.M.A. was everything a kid needed to be a hero in any combat situation. The ultimate weapon, the O.M.A. was more than three feet tall and weighed in at about four pounds (practically unheard of for an action toy of the time). It was the ultimate weapon that could be assembled and disassembled for whatever challenge the hero was facing.

This machine gun was an impressive weapon indeed. Its accoutrements—all fully operational, of course—included a grenade launcher, an antitank rocket, antibunker missiles, and a repeating rifle that could fire twelve plastic bullets in quick succession. Remove the stock, and you have a shorter tommy gun, and a pistol fit snugly under the rifle stock. It even came with a tripod stand for land battles. Oh, and, when you fired the rifle or the tommy gun, it made "realistic" shooting sounds. Kids who remember playing with it remember feeling invincible—and ready for any backyard military maneuvers.

WHERE IS IT NOW?

In the years that followed, other combat-ready toys appeared on the scene, but as Vietnam War fervor morphed into Cold War paranoia, and kids began to pretend to be secret agents rather than military troops, the toy weapons business shifted more to spy-related gear, and the O.M.A. was left behind.

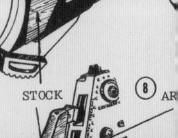

STOCK

8 AR

R

2

GRE
REL

While it's virtually impossible to conceive of parents buying their kids something like the O.M.A. today, the basic play pattern has lived on in such popular lines as the Power Rangers and the Transformers—not to mention in World of Warcraft and other multiplayer video combat games. In his wonderful and insight-ful book, *Killing Monsters: Why Kids Need Fantasy, Super-Heroes and Make-Believe Violence*, Gerard Jones argues that the kind of play that the Johnny Seven O.M.A. inspired builds self-confidence. By imagining themselves as heroes, kids prepare themselves to take on the more quotidian challenges of the grown-up world.

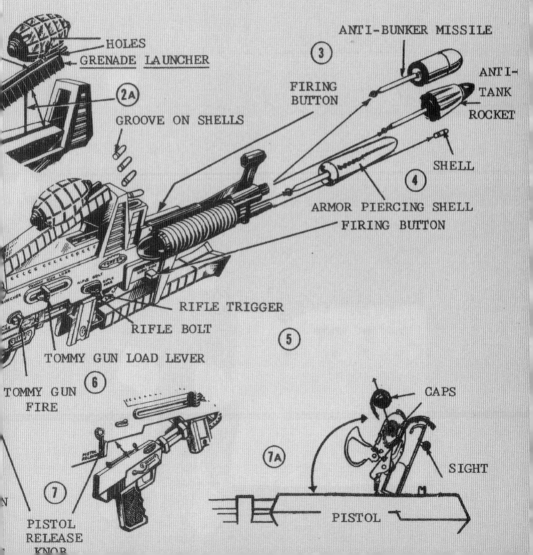

HOLES
GRENADE LAUNCHER

(2A)

GROOVE ON SHELLS

ANTI-BUNKER MISSILE

(3)

FIRING BUTTON

ANTI-TANK ROCKET

SHELL

(4)

ARMOR PIERCING SHELL
FIRING BUTTON

RIFLE TRIGGER
RIFLE BOLT

(5)

TOMMY GUN LOAD LEVER

TOMMY GUN FIRE

(6)

(7)

PISTOL RELEASE KNOB

(7A)

CAPS

SIGHT

PISTOL

Major Matt Mason 1966

Two years after Hasbro's mega-success with G.I. Joe, Mattel was scrambling to get into the new market of boys' action figures. Unfortunately, Hasbro had staked their claim on the four branches of military service with Joe, and the small company Rosko Industries had cornered the sports action figure market with their athletic Johnny Hero doll. (Johnny could be adapted for virtually any sport by changing his uniform and attaching accessories to a post in his hand.)

So what 1960s-era male hero was left?

Space explorer!

With the United States in the midst of the race to the moon, there was nary a red-blooded young American male who didn't fantasize about becoming an astronaut when he grew up. Plus, with opposition to the Vietnam War ratcheting up, G.I. Joe

DID YOU KNOW?
Major Matt Mason made at least one real trip into space when, in 1998, he flew along with John Glenn on his final shuttle mission aboard the *Discovery*.

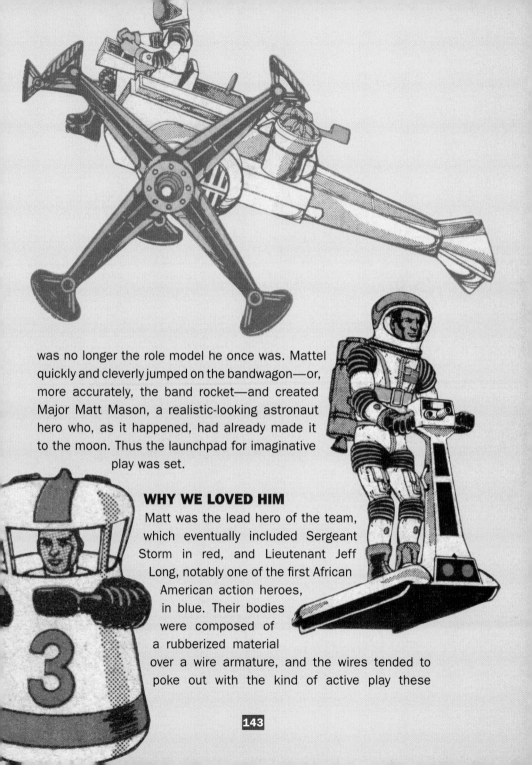

was no longer the role model he once was. Mattel quickly and cleverly jumped on the bandwagon—or, more accurately, the band rocket—and created Major Matt Mason, a realistic-looking astronaut hero who, as it happened, had already made it to the moon. Thus the launchpad for imaginative play was set.

WHY WE LOVED HIM

Matt was the lead hero of the team, which eventually included Sergeant Storm in red, and Lieutenant Jeff Long, notably one of the first African American action heroes, in blue. Their bodies were composed of a rubberized material over a wire armature, and the wires tended to poke out with the kind of active play these dolls inspired. But that didn't stop kids from loving them, in large part because they seemed so true to life. Cooler still, Mattel's designs for accessories such as the space helmet, the jet backpack, and the Space Crawler vehicle (all sold separately, of course) were based on actual NASA concept drawings that had been used in NASA publicity and were familiar to both kids and adults. Other realistic play sets included a three-level Space Station and a variety of vehicles.

WHERE IS HE NOW?

The major has made appearances in movies and TV shows, including *Stargate* and *The Wedding Singer*. In 1996, Matt made his off-Broadway debut in Kenneth Lonergan's *This Is Our Youth* (with Josh Hamilton and Mark Ruffalo).

In the early 1970s, after real astronauts finally reached the moon and interest in the space program lagged, Mattel tried to revitalize Matt and his space adventures by introducing a variety of aliens and action/adventure story lines, but by then kids had moved on. Still, the toy has an almost cultlike following among space enthusiasts and science fiction fans.

Because the rubberized body tended to degrade over time and, as noted, the wires would pop through with tough play, mint condition figures are somewhat rare, though they are available through eBay and other collector's sites. Compared to those of other action figures of the time, Matt's fan base is small, but they are no less passionate about the intergalactic adventures they shared.

In 2012, Robert Zemeckis and Tom Hanks, whose fascination with space is well known, announced they were trying to get a movie based on Matt off the ground. Perhaps this will launch a classic hero into the hearts and minds of a new generation.

FUN FACT:
The actual prop used in the play *This Is Our Youth* was really a Sergeant Storm figure that had belonged to my own younger brother! I never got it back for him after the show closed, and he's never let me forget it.

JET MATTEL'S MAJOR MATT MASON
AND ALL THIS NEAT EQUIPMENT!

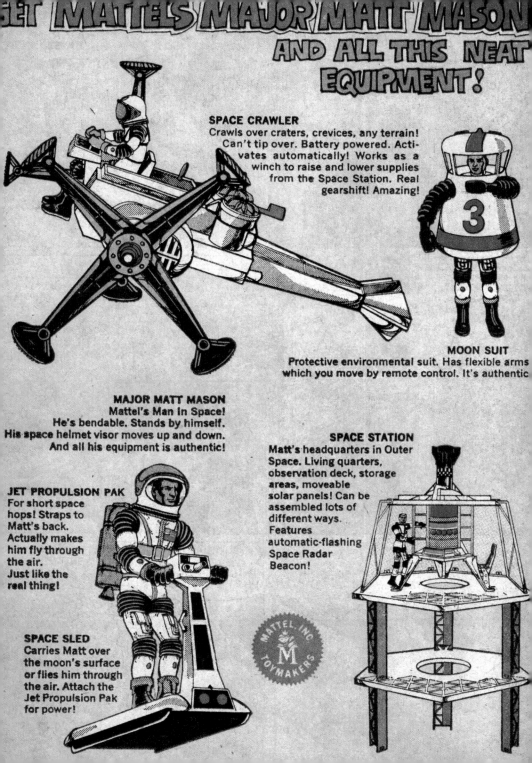

SPACE CRAWLER
Crawls over craters, crevices, any terrain! Can't tip over. Battery powered. Activates automatically! Works as a winch to raise and lower supplies from the Space Station. Real gearshift! Amazing!

MOON SUIT
Protective environmental suit. Has flexible arms which you move by remote control. It's authentic

MAJOR MATT MASON
Mattel's Man In Space! He's bendable. Stands by himself. His space helmet visor moves up and down. And all his equipment is authentic!

JET PROPULSION PAK
For short space hops! Straps to Matt's back. Actually makes him fly through the air. Just like the real thing!

SPACE STATION
Matt's headquarters in Outer Space. Living quarters, observation deck, storage areas, moveable solar panels! Can be assembled lots of different ways. Features automatic-flashing Space Radar Beacon!

SPACE SLED
Carries Matt over the moon's surface or flies him through the air. Attach the Jet Propulsion Pak for power!

MATTEL, INC. TOYMAKERS

Hot Wheels 1968

In 1968, Americans' romance with the automobile was at an all-time high. Muscle cars, sports cars—any kind of *fast* car, really—were all the rage and represented the freedom, power, and adventure of the '60s zeitgeist.

In the mid-1960s Matchbox cars had been the epitome of toy car fun, but as real cars began to go faster, Matchbox began to seem tame—at least for kids who were looking for a little more action. Luckily, Elliot Handler, one of the founders of Mattel, saw that what boys wanted in their toy cars was speed . . . and more speed. Throw in a few daring stunts and a death-defying leap from the kitchen table to the countertop, and that was a peak play experience.

But to get that kind of speed in a toy car, Handler and his team had to innovate. Instead of attaching wheels directly to the body of the car, as was standard at the time, Mattel added an axle and "frictionless" plastic wheels. This simple design improve-ment created a toy car that could go faster than any before it.

WHY WE LOVED THEM

The very first Hot Wheels car rolled off the production line in 1968. It was the Custom Camaro, and it was significant not just because it was the first in the Hot Wheels brand but because it was the first time that consumers would see a car in minia-ture *before* General Motors released a real version. This was true for all

sixteen cars introduced in the line's debut year.

Hot Wheels cars were a huge and immediate hit, earning the new brand notoriety for both the integrity of its replicas and the imagination in its concepts. Adulation grew when Mattel introduced its now iconic orange track system, which was a first—and took the play to a whole new level. For the growing number of fans, this was the best yet. Complete with launchers such as the power booster, which used foam wheels to shoot the cars along the track, Hot Wheels ran Matchbox off the road and quickly became the toy cars that kids had to have.

WHERE ARE THEY NOW?

With nearly three billion cars sold, Hot Wheels remains one of the biggest toy brands in the United States. Mattel introduces more than two hundred new models every year, and has expanded the brand to include other high-performance vehicles and special series—including reintroductions of classic favorites. Hot Wheels collecting and history have inspired books, websites, and conventions.

SSP Racers 1970

They howled with power. At least that's what the commercial said. They were also enhanced with "sonic sound," which, despite its redundancy, communicated awesome speed to the legions of boys who embraced SSP Racers with a passion. Chalk up one more winning design to Marvin Glass, who dreamed up these pint-sized powerhouses.

WHY WE LOVED THEM

SSP Racers were all about going *fast*. The body of the car had an integrated rubber flywheel that was operated by a T-stick ripcord. The teeth on the T-stick engaged a cog on the side of the fly-wheel, and when it was pulled—or "ripped"—it sent the wheel spinning and the car streaking out at high speed. Better yet, the flywheel was strategically balanced in each car so that its plastic body could sail above the sidewalk—or wherever the high-speed race was happening.

The cars could do stunts, bash, crash, and still come back for more. While kids could play alone for hours on end with Matchbox cars and Hot Wheels, the SSP cars were all about competition. The challenge was to pull the T-stick harder than your opponent in head-to-head races. Part of the fun was building obstacles and ramps and challenging your opponents to all kinds of dangerous stunts. But these things were well built, and they stood up to all the stuff kids could dish out.

The car wasn't without its dangers, however. Many a kid burned their fingers (though not severely) from touching the spinning flywheel. You could also get a burn if you held the car from the bottom and pulled the T-stick . . . if your palm was in the way. Ouch.

WHERE ARE THEY NOW?

As the popularity of the SSP Racers grew, Kenner began to release different sets, including a memorable favorite: a demolition derby with breakaway pieces.

By the end of the 1970s, however, the craze had slowed down. Hot Wheels stunt sets were still hot, but skateboarding was rapidly becoming the neighborhood race game of choice.

It's unlikely that the SSP would be brought back today, but its true innovation—the T-stick ripcord—has powered any number of toys since. Mattel's 1984 He-Man Road Ripper, for example, was charged not, sad to say, by "the power of Grayskull" but by a plastic ripcord. And Hasbro's current Beyblade line of battling tops uses the T-stick ripcord as well. So while the SSP Racers may have sped off into the sunset, their legacy drives on.

The Six Million Dollar Man 1975

Gentlemen, we can rebuild him. We have the technology. We have the capability to make the world's first bionic man."

If you were around from 1974 to 1978, you probably welcomed those familiar words into your home every week as your family nuked some TV dinners and gathered around the television to watch the latest installment of *The Six Million Dollar Man*. For more than one hundred episodes and through several TV movies, millions of viewers immersed themselves in the adventures of astronaut Steve Austin as he battled evil using his unstoppable bionic powers.

WHY WE LOVED HIM

If ever there was a story line made for boys in the mid-1970s, this was it. In the wake of Skylab and the Voyager missions, astronauts had become akin to real-life superheroes. At the same time, the home computer was becoming a reality, and people were fascinated by the new technology. Add to that a character who cheated death to become the toughest guy around, and a contemporary hero with a classic twist was born.

The twelve-inch Steve Austin action figure had a bionic arm complete with a roll-up sleeve to show where his wiring had been replaced, and painted "circuit blocks" kids could take in and out. When you turned his head and pumped the switch on his back (powering a rudimentary hydraulic), the bionic man would lift up an enormous engine block (included). When his arms got tired from all that lifting, you could simply take them out and swap in an extra pair (not included).

Far and away the most popular feature, though, was the bionic eye. It didn't do much, but kids could look through it and *pretend* to have bionic vision, and that was enough. It was all about the imagination.

The Steve Austin figure was the centerpiece of the line, and the most popular, but as the show—as well as demand from kids—exploded over the next three years, more toys and characters followed. There were at least three different versions of the Steve Austin figure, and Steve Austin's boss, Oscar Goldman, got his own toy, as did Big Foot and Austin's arch nemesis Maskatron. There were also play sets and spaceships, of course, so kids could re-create the whole intergalactic world of Steve Austin.

WHERE IS HE NOW?

As so often happens, by the time the show was canceled in 1978, the kids who had made the toys such a hit had grown out of them. But a bigger threat was on the horizon as well—a little movie called *Star Wars*.

When Kenner introduced its three-and-three-fourths-inch *Star Wars* action figures in 1977 (less than half the size of the Bionic Man), and Hasbro soon followed suit with a relaunch of a smaller G.I. Joe, it was the end of an era for the Six Million Dollar Man and other large action toys.

Of course, collectors still love them, and mint condition figures can go for as much as $500 in the original packaging, though in most cases, the plastic sleeve covering the bionic features has dried out and disintegrated over time, making a fully functioning toy a definite rarity.

Still, while most collectibles eventually lose their superpowers, bionic memories refuse to die.

Stretch Armstrong 1976

This muscled he-man had blond hair and wore nothing but his wrestling briefs. For kids, the promise that his limbs could stretch to *four times their original size* afforded hours of delight and play. Could he do it? Can I do it? And, of course, can I stretch him even *more*? After all, there's something satisfying about tests of strength and endurance, particularly when kids get to fantasize about having superior strength and power themselves. And indeed, many a kid measured his or her strength (Stretch had plenty of girl fans) by the ability to push Stretch's limits.

HOW WE PLAYED WITH HIM

Naturally, Stretch had to be quite durable to stand up to this type of play. He was made of latex and filled with—believe it or not—corn syrup. This made him vulnerable to punctures, but a bit of tape, an inner tube patch or a Band-Aid could usually make him right again. Those who played with Stretch will recall some of their more innovative attempts to stretch him—whether by using him

for tug-of-war or running him over with a bike, car, or perhaps even a lawnmower. Stretch tended not to endure these attempts very well, but they did at least create enduring memories.

WHERE IS HE NOW?

As toys go, Stretch had a pretty good run, hanging around until the early 1980s. In 1993, when professional wrestling was in its heyday, Cap Toys saw an opportunity to relaunch Stretch (though this time he was filled with tiny beads instead of corn syrup–based gel). However, though Stretch may have always snapped back to his original size, he never quite snapped back to his former glory.

Given the beatings he took, it's no surprise Stretch toys didn't age well. Plus, the latex and gel dried out over time, and owners of the original recall what happened if he was left in a hot car. (Not pretty.) So originals still in good condition are extremely rare and command a high price among collectors.

Hasbro, who has owned the prop-

erty since its acquisition of Cap Toys, has had a feature film based on Stretch in the works since 2008, and at this writing Hollywood rumors suggest it may debut in 2014. If it does, it's sure to (wait for it) stretch out his lifespan at least another few years.

Star Wars Action Figures 1977

What can anyone say about *Star Wars* that hasn't been said? There has never been a movie franchise that has been so thoroughly discussed and dissected. *Star Wars* completely transformed popular culture and, with it, the toy business.

Before *Star Wars*, there was no such thing as the adult action figure collector. Today, there are legions of avid collectors who scour vintage toy stores, auction houses, and old garages all over the globe for the most obscure figures from the movies, TV shows, and comic books alike—and it all began with *Star Wars*.

Yet the potential for toy tie-ins was not immediately obvious to toy companies; after all, *Star Wars* was not a children's movie. Mego, the leading company for action figures at the time, passed on the opportunity to make *Star Wars* toys, as did Mattel. Kenner began production of the *Star Wars* characters several months after the movie premiered because the agreement to create them had been signed just prior to the film's opening. For the holiday season of 1977, Kenner sold empty boxes as a promise that the figures were on the way. It was controversial at the time, but it's a legendary study in marketing, as they sold more than 600,000 of those empty packages. (*Star*

Wars also changed the entire way toys based on movies were created. Once an afterthought, toy deals are now signed before the scripts are even finished.)

By today's standards, those original figures were somewhat crude. To produce them in the then-new three-and-three-fourths-inch size, detail was sacrificed. The faces looked little like the actors, and though the figures' arms and legs moved, movements were stiff and clumsy.

It turned out that none of this mattered, as *Star Wars* created a passion—in some cases an obsession—among kids and adults alike that's never been matched.

As each new film was released, more characters joined the pantheon and new fans discovered the stories. Yet as popular as they were, *Star Wars* action figures never became a fad. They were something better: a reliable franchise that was regularly extended and carefully managed to keep the characters alive in the hearts and minds of its fans.

WHERE ARE THEY NOW?

There is no age limit for *Star Wars* fans, and many original collectors have passed their treasures on to their children, many of whom have added to the collections. In fact, the third generation of *Star Wars* fans is just getting old enough to be introduced to the stories and characters, and the joy of coming across that rare Vinyl Caped Jawa on eBay.

But while *Star Wars* action figures continue to be big business, they are no longer the only toys in town. In 1999, LEGO launched its first *Star Wars* kit—the original X-Wing Starfighter—and in in 2008, *Star Wars: The Clone Wars* debuted in theaters and on television, creating new story lines that required a whole new line of toys.

DID YOU KNOW?
Thirty-six years after the original movie's release, it's estimated that as of 2012, approximately 2,300 unique *Star Wars* action figures have been created.

He-Man and Masters of the Universe 1981

I n the early 1980s, playgrounds and backyards rang with the cries of boys invoking "The Power of Grayskull." No question about it, He-Man and Masters of the Universe (MOTU, to the cognoscenti) offered the ultimate fantasy for kids of any era—unstoppable superhero powers. Now the kid picked last for dodgeball could transform himself into an impressively muscled master of the universe—at least in the world of his imagination.

WHY WE LOVED HIM

The basic story line was nothing new. Using his mythic powers, the gentle Prince Adam morphs into He-Man, battles the evil villains, and saves all of mankind. New or not, the toy line and the TV show, which premiered in 1983, were two of the biggest hits of the decade. But they might not have caught on had it not been for *Star Wars*. In the late 1960s, Mattel had made an epic blunder by failing to adapt its action toys to the space era, surrendering the boys' action figure market to Kenner and Hasbro. The company was ready for a revival when they finally hit on this combination of comic book adventure and classic action toy.

DID YOU KNOW?

Tom Wolfe appropriated the phrase "Masters of the Universe" for his 1987 satire *The Bonfire of the Vanities*.

After years of relatively static action figures (with the exception of G.I. Joe's Kung-Fu Grip), Mattel came back swinging (literally) with the He-Man "Power Punch." Twist this winsome warrior at the waist, and his bulging biceps would deliver a rubber-band-driven right hook to the evil Skeletor.

In 1985, in an attempt to attract a broader market

(and stave off accusations of sexism among would-be heroines), Prince Adam (He-Man's alter ego) discovered he had a twin sister named Adora, who became She-Ra, Princess of Power. Though Wonder Woman had paved the way in the late 1970s, She-Ra was the first female action hero to be played with equally by both boys *and* girls. But this was only the beginning of Mattel's quest for world domination. During this first wave of MOTU popularity, more than 150 characters and play sets were produced, and kids clamored to collect them all.

The early 1980s were the heyday of the play set—large plastic castles or villages or worlds where stories came to life—and the MOTU line was no exception. (Play sets were always among the most profitable for toy companies, and the most heavily advertised on TV.) The prized jewel for He-Man fans was Castle Grayskull, which rivaled Barbie's Dream House in size and features, including a working elevator, drawbridge, and trapdoor. It's one of the most widely remembered toys by adults who had it (and many who didn't, but coveted it).

WHERE ARE THEY NOW?

The original MOTU toys had a very long run, from 1981 to 1987. Starting with comic books in 1981 and expanding to TV and movies in 1983, the various story lines kept kids engaged for six years before MOTU started to fade. But children of the '80s hadn't seen the last of He-Man.

In 2008, Mattel turned to the design group Four Horsemen to redesign the figures for a new generation—or at least for collectors, who still love the line. While the new generation MOTU have become popular collectibles, the originals, too, are still coveted. In a particularly modern twist on old-school nostalgia, there are even iPhone apps to connect collectors and track down the now highly prized original figures.

Transformers 1984

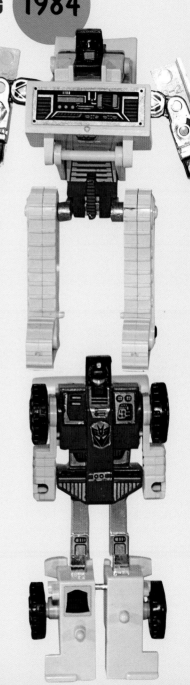

In the early 1980s, transforming robots weren't a new concept. They had been popular in Japan, but the story lines weren't very well developed, and they never really translated to the American market.

That is, until Hasbro brought together the different lines under the Transformers banner and developed the story of Optimus Prime, the good guy leader of the Autobots, and Megatron, the nefarious villain who commanded the evil Decepticons.

WHY WE LOVED THEM

Yes, transforming the robots from a vehicle to a robot and back again was fun, but what sealed the deal with the kids was the story line, established through a TV series and a popular comic book so that by the time the toys rolled into stores in 1984, they had already captured boys' imaginations.

The first series featured battles between eighteen Autobots and ten Decepticons, and they touched off real-life battles of their own as holiday shoppers waged war in toy store aisles to secure the quickly sold-out toys. As this came only a year after the Cabbage Patch slugfests, the yearly competition to score "the hot new toy" had entered the culture for good.

As we've seen again and again, success breeds imitation, and the market was suddenly flooded with a variety of knock-offs. In fact, so many fake transformers hit the market that in 1985 Hasbro put a special badge on its official merchandise. When activated by the heat of a finger, the badge would show an Autobot or Decepticon logo—proof that the kid had an authentic Transformer. It was the epitome of cool at the time.

The TV series, which drove the story and toy sales, lasted through 1987, and the 1986 animated movie was a huge hit. The death of Optimus Prime at the end of the movie—a risky gambit, to be sure—prompted an unprecedented letter-writing campaign to Hasbro, but fortunately, robots can't die in the traditional sense, and Optimus was reanimated to fight another day.

Throughout the 1980s, many new models of varying complexity were introduced, including the innovative spring-loaded self-transforming toys and Transformers for younger children (marketed under Hasbro's Playskool brand). Of course, the story line got only more and more robust.

WHERE ARE THEY NOW?

Transfomers remain a powerhouse toy line for Hasbro. With three hit movies—and a fourth on the way

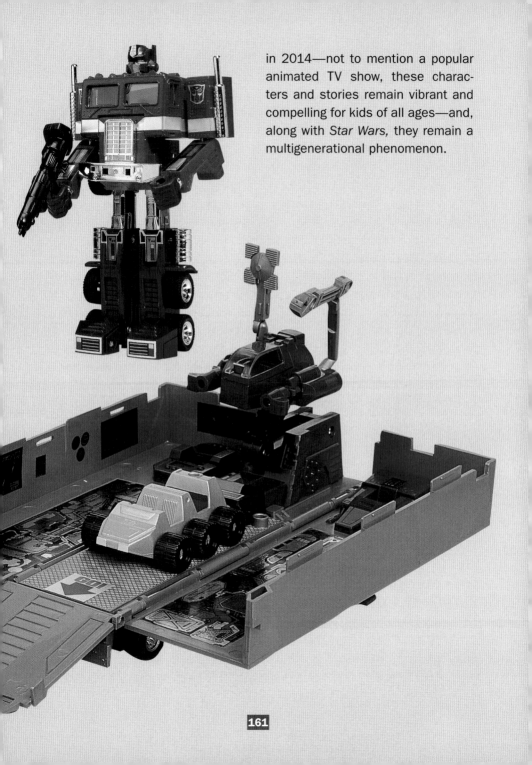

in 2014—not to mention a popular animated TV show, these characters and stories remain vibrant and compelling for kids of all ages—and, along with *Star Wars,* they remain a multigenerational phenomenon.

MicroMachines 1986

If little is cool, then tiny must be cooler . . . or so one might assume, considering the popularity of MicroMachines in the mid-1980s. These ultratiny cars were about half the size of a typical Hot Wheels or Matchbox car (they had a scale ratio of approximately 1:152), but for kids of the '80s, they provided an equally large dose of fun.

WHY WE LOVED THEM

MicroMachines were created by Clem Heeden, who licensed the idea to Galoob. Over the next several years, Galoob hit the figurative gas and rolled out millions of the teeny vehicles, from cars and trucks to airplanes, speedboats, motorcycles, monster trucks, and military vehicles, to name just a few. There were also countless tracks and play sets that could be configured and combined to create an entire superhighway system for these tiny cars.

There were also MicroMachines cars modeled on hot entertainment franchises, including the Mighty Morphin Power Rangers, *Star Trek*, James Bond, and Indiana Jones. But probably the most popular—and most remembered to this day—was the line based on *Star Wars*.

They were such a hit that they made MicroMachines the most popular toy car on the market for several years, cutting off both Hot Wheels and Matchbox on the inside turn.

But the thing that really kicked MicroMachines into high gear was the now classic TV commercial featuring John Moschitta, Jr., at the time the world's fastest talker (clocking in at 586 words per minute, according to Guinness World Records). The fun of trying to decipher his speed-talking gibberish kept kids listening, entertained, and clamoring for more MicroMachines.

DID YOU KNOW?

MicroMachines were used as a defensive weapon in the movie *Home Alone* when Kevin McCallister (Macaulay Culkin) tripped up the invading thieves with a phalanx of MicroMachines scattered at the bottom of a staircase.

WHEN DID THEY PUT ON THE BRAKES?

After Hasbro acquired the brand in 1998, the cars largely went off the market. There are MicroMachines conspiracy theories on the Internet that imply that Hasbro was trying to kill any competition to their *Star Wars* toys, but that should be taken with the same grain of salt that most online conspiracy theories deserve. More likely, it was the rise of video games that put these cars up on blocks.

In recent years, more companies have been producing microminiature cars, and while some of them are excellent toys, no one brand has captured the imagination the way MicroMachines did.

Teenage Mutant Ninja Turtles 1988

Now here's an unlikely group of heroes: teenage turtles who talk like surfers, fight like ninjas, play rock and roll, and subsist primarily on pizza. Doesn't sound very mainstream, does it?

Well, it wasn't. The Teenage Mutant Ninja Turtles came from under ground, literally. But I don't just mean the sewer where they lived. The ninja turtles got their start in a series of underground comic books created by Kevin Eastman and Peter Laird in 1984.

Interestingly, the four classically named characters—Michelangelo, Leonardo, Donatello, and Raphael (the creators studied art history in college)—were originally designed to satirize the whole action figure / superhero genre. Tired of their uninspiring jobs, they invested about $1,200 to produce three thousand black-and-white copies of their first comic book. It quickly became a hit in the underground comic world. Pretty soon they were selling more than 1,500 copies of each issue—the most successful black-and-white comic of all time.

As often happens in the toy business, anytime new characters start to attract an audience (even if that audience is comic book nerds living in their parents' basement), people start to pay attention. One of those people was Mark Freedman, who owned a relatively small company at the time and was des-

WHY WE LOVED THEM

Now, had Eastman and Laird studied child development instead of art history, they might have predicted what would happen next. Young kids, the audience for both afternoon cartoons and action figures, don't really get satire. Instead, they simply thought that any amphibians who could karate chop the heck out of street thugs, evil overlords, and alien invaders—*and* knew how to surf—were very cool. They also loved the jokey camaraderie of the turtles, who were the kind of irreverent and funny teens young boys aspired to be—that is, if they lived in sewers and had been trained in martial arts by a mutated rat named Splinter. Plus, kids universally love talking animals (just ask Disney).

perate for a piece of the boys' action figure business. He snapped up the property and brought the turtles from the black-and-white world of underground comics to the very colorful world of mass-market toys. And since this was the 1980s, a time when no toy succeeded without a TV show, a pilot was produced before you could say "Cowabunga."

But we also loved them for how they spoke. Suddenly people who had never seen a "killer wave" were shouting "Cowabunga!" on a daily or even hourly basis (much to the chagrin of many a teacher and parent). In fact, though it may be hard for children of the '80s to recall a time when the word "dude" wasn't part of the common vocabulary, its prevalence in our culture today is largely attributable to the Turtles.

They had a farther-reaching impact, as well. Interest in martial arts exploded, and pizza sales soared through the roof.

WHERE ARE THEY NOW?

Inevitably, the fad passed and the Power Rangers and other newer action heroes replaced the Turtles. However, in 2012, Nickelodeon decided to bring them back out of their shells with a new, slightly more modern version of the original show (and, of course, the requisite line of merchandise, comics, and games), and once again the Turtles are riding the A-frame. "Cowabunga!"

Chapter 7

For Two to Four Players

There was once a time when board games were a quiet pastime. Players sat around a board, rolled the dice, moved their markers around, and someone eventually won. It was all very civilized. Well, that all changed as the skill-and-action game was born.

While the classic board games never went away, it was the introduction of Mouse Trap in 1963 that kicked games into high gear. Suddenly, games were no longer placid, sit-around-a-table-and-play-nice affairs; now there was movement, activity, and tons and tons of noise. Games became boisterous and sometimes even frenetic. Much laughter—and more than a little bit of heckling—ensued. (My brothers and I were especially adept at turning any game into a contact sport—even the relatively sedentary classics Monopoly, Sorry!, and Risk.)

One of the things that set these games apart was how TV-friendly they were, and indeed TV commercials played a huge role in the proliferation of these explosive games. With the rise of television, marketers could show all the loud, chaotic fun of a game in progress. (One notable similarity of these commercials was that the games usually ended with Dad on the losing end. Hey, what kid wouldn't want to challenge and best good old Dad, even if it was only in a game?)

Prolific inventor Marvin Glass was behind several of these games—many of which are still made today. The game category would be reinvented again with the introduction of role-playing games that created entire subcultures of fans—think Dungeons and Dragons—in the mid-1970s.

What's always set the most popular games apart has been that there really is no other comparable play experience, and that's why they endure. The best of them are both easy to learn and different every time they're played, which is why so many of them have endured into the digital age.

Today, perhaps as a response to all the digital entertainment, skill and action games are experiencing a resurgence, with the classics attracting a new generation of kids, and inventors once again coming up with new ways to make lots of noise—and fun—with board games. While life may never be quite the same as it was in the days before Atari and Nintendo gaming systems, board games are still an exceptional social experience, and adults who remember when their families could spend hours playing Operation or Ker-Plunk or Twister or Mystery Date are only too happy to keep playing.

Nok Hockey *c.1942*

I n the post–World War II years, street hockey became a neighborhood fixture in cities and in the growing suburbs. But not every day was one for playing outside. Enter Carrom with Nok Hockey, a tabletop version of the outdoor street game.

WHY WE LOVED IT

It was a simple toy: a box with a particleboard bottom, two plastic sticks, and a couple of wooden discs, and this simplicity was part of its appeal. The ingenious design innovation was nothing more than two diamond-shaped blocks of wood guarding the goals, which were slots at the narrow ends of the game's Goal Zones that let the discs shoot out of the box.

Like its outdoor counterpart, the fun of this game was the controlled mayhem. Oh, and noise. Whether it was the kids shouting and cheer-

ing or the slamming of the sticks against the wood, this was not quiet play.

Plus, there were no rules. Well, there were some instructions, but Carrom more or less left everything up to the kids, who were only too eager to create "house rules." Over the years, there was some standardization of the play, but nothing has ever been "official." This game wasn't about rules. It was all about the action.

WHERE IS IT NOW?

Nok Hockey was the inspiration and precursor to air hockey and electronic hockey games, but today you can buy a Nok Hockey set virtually identical to the one first made more than sixty years ago. The longevity of this simple game is a testament to the fact that the play is almost always more important than the toy itself.

Cootie 1948

It's a playground taunt as old as playgrounds themselves: "You've got cooties!" How many generations of kids have shrieked those fateful words, pretending to give themselves cootie shots while running away from the playground outcast rumored to be afflicted?

So it was perhaps only a matter of time before that became a game, created by Herb Schaper as early as 1948. A simple, luck-based racing game, it didn't have a game board (which was rare for games at the time). The single objective was to be the first to assemble one's adorable, plastic Cootie Bug by rolling a die to determine what part went on next.

At first, Schaper could barely give away this weird boardless game, so he convinced the local Dayton's department store to sell it on consignment. But like any playground bug, it soon caught on, and by the early 1950s, the game had become a staple in many homes and preschools, and remained so for decades.

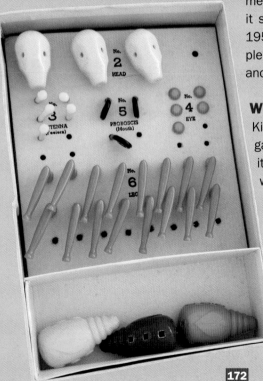

WHY WE LOVED IT

Kids who remember playing the game may also recall how much fun it was to do the "Cootie Dance"—which involved jumping around screaming and scratching as if you had contracted actual cooties yourself.

WHERE IS IT NOW?

The game is still being made and sold, and kids continue to threaten cootie infestations on playgrounds everywhere.

COOTIE

TRADE MARK REG.
PAT. PEND.

AN EXCITING EDUCATIONAL GAME FOR ALL AGES

DID YOU KNOW?
The 1975 Macy's Thanksgiving Day parade featured a fifteen-foot-tall Cootie Bug float.

FUN FACT:
In 1986, Rob Angel couldn't get anyone to buy his little game called Pictionary. He convinced Nordstrom department store in Seattle to take it on consignment, too. And, like Cootie, it became very popular.

Mouse Trap 1963

I t wasn't a better mousetrap that Milton Glass set out to build in 1963, it was a better board game. Sure, Monopoly, Clue, Sorry!, and other classics were all big hits, but the iconoclastic game designer couldn't help but wonder what would happen if he combined toylike elements with a board game. His inspirations were the kooky Rube Goldberg contraptions featured in the *Inventions* cartoons

that had been appearing regularly in newspapers since 1914. So ubiquitous were these cartoons, in fact, that by the early 1960s, "Rube Goldberg" had entered the American lexicon as a way of describing anything that used maximum effort to achieve minimal results. What could be better inspiration for a board-game-meets-toy?

HOW WE PLAYED IT

The ultimate goal of the game was to keep your mouse out of the trap, but the fun was in building a mousetrap that worked. Players took turns adding pieces to the contraption as they moved their mice playing pieces around the board. When the trap was finally built, you didn't want to land on the "Cheese" space when another player landed on the "Turn Crank" space, for that was his or her opportunity to set the machine going. Balls

174

would roll, hands would swing, levers would be pushed, and if all went according to plan, a basket would drop, trapping your mouse, and you would be out of the game.

But like any true Rube Goldberg device, effective operation wasn't always guaranteed. Half the fun of the game was that even when built correctly, the contraption could misfire—and the game would continue. Eventually, there would be one player left who had avoided the trap, and he or she would be declared the winner.

WHY WE LOVED IT

What made this game so appealing was its silliness and the unpredictability. But the advertising didn't hurt, either; the zany TV commercials depicting the action of the game, combined with the popularity of the Rube Goldberg cartoons, made this one of the bestselling games of the year.

The success of Mouse Trap signaled the beginning of the golden age of skill-and-action games, inspiring such favorites as Crazy Clock, Booby Trap, Dynamite Shack, Time Bomb, Battling Tops, Tip It, Toss Across, Fascination, and many more. Whether the game involved racing the clock, balancing disks on a swinging tower, or throwing beanbags against a board, the fun was always in the controlled chaos.

WHERE IS IT NOW?

Of all the skill-and-action games it inspired, Mouse Trap has arguably had the greatest staying power. It's still made today. Like classic comedy, the silly game play and the unpredictable outcomes are the kinds of things people never get tired of. And really, who can look at this crazy contraption and not get a good laugh?

Crazy Clock

The toy industry has always worked on the premise that if something is good, more of it is better. That pretty much mimics a seven-year-old's perception of the world, too, and sometimes it pays off. The toy business also demands new stuff every year. Particularly in the 1960s, having that new item to put on TV was important to keep up with the competition.

Given the tremendous success of Mouse Trap, Ideal went back to Marvin Glass for another Rube Goldberg–type game, and the result was Crazy Clock. Perhaps inspired by Goldberg's drawing "A Simple Alarm Clock," Glass set out to create a contraption that when assembled would eject a little plastic sleeping man from his bed.

For this game, Glass got rid of the game board and used cards to take players through the process of building the contraption. If all went according to plan, when the clock was built, and a player got to wind it, a broom would knock a ball down some stairs that would set some feet running down the track that would kick a golf ball that ran down a chute to hit a man that activated a bird and dropped an egg out of a nest onto a tilting pool table that made a candle swing and woke up your sleeper.

Like Mouse Trap, the mechanics didn't work every time, and that added tension to the game, because if the machine was a dud, the chance to wind the clock would pass to the next player.

WHAT HAPPENED?

The commercial did a great job of selling kids on the game—the same kids who had clamored for Mouse Trap the year before—but in actual play

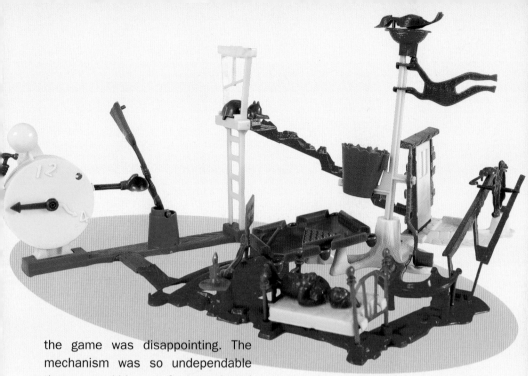

the game was disappointing. The mechanism was so undependable that many kids got frustrated and stopped playing. In the mid-1960s, parents didn't automatically return something that didn't work as expected, so Ideal did pretty well with the game. But it only really lasted one year.

Ideal did one more Rube Goldberg–inspired game called Fish Bait in 1965, but by that time the trend and the interest had passed. (It also didn't work all that well.) Ideal introduced Tip It the same year, and that one became a classic.

Cardinal tried to reissue the game in 2000 under the name Wake Up Sam, presumably to compete with the 1992 Parker Brothers game

Don't Wake Daddy that had become a consistent seller, but it didn't take off. Cardinal presumably had acquired the molds and the rights to the game after the breakup of CBS Toys (which had purchased Ideal in 1982) in 1986.

WHERE ARE THEY NOW?

Crazy Clock remains merely a memory for those who played with it. There are some older versions around as collectibles, but those mostly don't work. The springs and other pieces of the mechanism invariably got lost, so it would be rare to find a fully functional Crazy Clock game today.

Green Ghost 1965

One of the earliest glow-in-the-dark toys was called Fireball, a ball that had glow-in-the-dark liquid—made out of the compound zinc sulfide—inside. After charging it up in the light, kids swirled the liquid to coat the inside of the ball—thus enabling them to play catch in the dark.

By the mid-1960s, manufacturers had figured out how to mold the chemical into plastic to achieve this effect. The glowing Frisbee soon followed, and in 1965, Transogram introduced the first glow-in-the dark board game, Green Ghost.

HOW WE PLAYED IT

Designed to be played in the dark, the plastic game board was elevated on six legs, so no table or surface was needed (one less thing to bump into). Before play, the board and all the glowing elements had to be "charged." That is, they had to have strong light shone on them so they would glow when the lights were turned out.

The board, not surprisingly, depicted a graveyard, and each player was one of the Green Ghost's pets, sent to travel around the board and retrieve twelve little ghosts (all named after shades of green) locked in the three crypts. The object of the game was to be the player who found Kelly Green as they searched for him (or her) in the crypts. Players had to avoid bones, bat feathers, and snakes, and the game board had holes in it that your piece could "disappear" down and come up through another hole in the board. It was an ingenious variation on the standard chase game, and since you were in the dark, it played on touch rather than seeing and counting. When all the little ghosts had been collected, they were placed in the base of the spinner. The Green Ghost was given one more turn, and the ghost he ended up pointing at was determined to be Kelly, and the player who found it was the winner. Basically, the winner was determined by a random spin, which are lousy game mechanics, but kids didn't mind so much—the fun was in playing in the dark.

WHERE IS IT NOW?

The main problem with the game was that its glow—along with its novelty—would wear off if the play went on too long, so it had to constantly be recharged. It was also not really all that much fun to play before dark.

Still, today Green Ghost has a small following of fans, and even a Facebook page. There have been efforts to revitalize the title since 2009, but to date that hasn't happened.

No other complete glow-in-the-dark board games have been introduced since.

Mystery Date   1965

O pen the door for your . . . mystery date."

HOW WE PLAYED IT

That enticing offer was the gimmick behind this board game, designed by the prolific Marvin Glass for Milton Bradley. Mystery Date was targeted to girls ages six to fourteen, and play involved moving around the game board and collecting cards that pictured items of clothing the players might imagine wearing on their date. A full outfit took three cards, and players would keep drawing until satisfied they had the perfectly coordinated outfit.

Then came the moment of truth: When the player landed on the "Open Door" space, she would gingerly open the plastic front door in the middle of the board, revealing whether her date was a "dream" or a "dud." A dream date might be an athletic stud proposing a trip to the beach, or a well-groomed gent bearing a corsage and an invitation to a formal. The "dud," on the other hand, arrived looking sloppy and unshaven with no specific plans.

WHY WE LOVED IT

The game was right on trend. From *The Many Loves of Dobie Gillis* to *The Patty Duke Show,* the most popular TV shows of the time featured teens and their dating adventures. However, for girls who were too young to date but couldn't wait to be teenagers with legions of male suitors (or so they imagined), the game was a perfect way to play out that fantasy.

WHERE IS IT NOW?

The appeal of the game long outlasted the 1960s; it was reissued in 1970, and again in 1995 and 2005. With each new version,

TAKE 2 CARDS FROM DRAW PILE

SWAP 1 CARD WITH ANY PLAYER

TAKE 1 CARD FROM DRAW PILE

TAKE 1 CARD FROM DRAW OR DISCARD PILE

OPEN THE DOOR ?

SWAP 1 CARD WITH PLAYER ON RIGHT

the outfits and the dates both got a makeover to reflect more contemporary sensibilities.

Various versions of Mystery Date are still available, and the small game company Winning Moves sells a replica of the original. Women who remember playing with the original all say versions of the same thing: Even the guys considered duds in 1965 look better than a lot of the kids trying to date their daughters today. (Yeah, you did become your mother.)

Twister 1966

It was the phenomenon that almost wasn't.

It's hard to imagine, but as popular as Twister is, it was just one day—and one lucky break—away from being an also-ran. On the eve of its release, May 3, 1966, Milton Bradley got the news that Sears was canceling its order for the edgy new game, saying it wasn't appropriate for kids. Evidently, the folks in Milton Bradley's PR department didn't get the news in time. That night they took Twister to *The Tonight Show Starring Johnny Carson,* and Carson played it on air with Eva Gabor. Would there ever be a more hilarious way to debut a wacky new game?

FUN FACT:

On the thirtieth anniversary of the game in 1996, your author refereed a re-creation of the famous Johnny Carson—Eva Gabor match live on TV, though this time it was between Regis Philbin and Dolly Parton.

According to Milton Bradley, the next morning there was a line about fifty people deep in front of Abercrombie and Fitch in New York clamoring for the game. The word was out, and before long, stores—Sears included—were tying themselves in knots trying to restock the shelves fast enough. Twister had found its audience, but it wasn't little kids. Teens and adults drove the game's initial success, though kids were soon to follow.

WHY WE LOVED IT

Twister couldn't have been more perfect for the "swinging '60s." While there was nothing inherently sexual about the game, it reflected people's growing comfort with their bodies, sexual freedom, and the idea that it was perfectly fine for men and women to be tangled up together on a plastic sheet. It was a fun and innocent way for adults to be physically close, and it tapped in perfectly to the spirit of the times.

WHERE IS IT NOW?

The game continues to be popular, and although the original players may feel too stiff and inflexible to engage in the game, today's kids and young adults love it.

DID YOU KNOW?

Hasbro estimates that significantly more than twenty-five million Twister games have been sold since its introduction. That's a lot of people tying themselves up in knots.

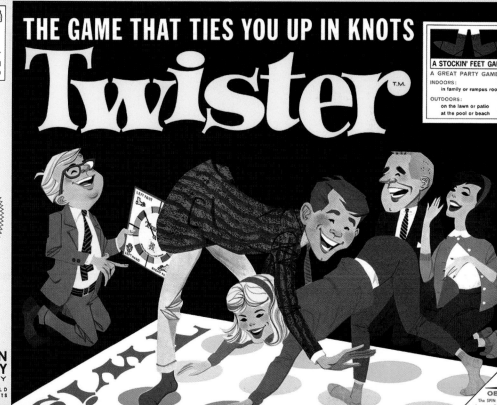

Rock 'Em Sock 'Em Robots 1966

Try this phrase on virtually any baby boomer: "My block is knocked off!" Immediately you'll conjure up memories of one of the most famous commercials of the mid-1960s. Those old enough to have seen it will fondly remember the thrill of watching Junior handily dispatch Dad as the Red Rocker squared off against the Blue Bomber in a large plastic boxing ring. (I could write an entire treatise on why Dad was always a doofus in the game commercials of this period, but never mind for now.)

WHY WE LOVED 'EM

Was there ever a more hilarious way for boys to channel their inherent aggression than battle by plastic robot? And parents liked it, too, because no one actually got hurt; it was, in other words, an acceptable way for kids to brawl.

This was not a sophisticated or precise toy. Handles on the

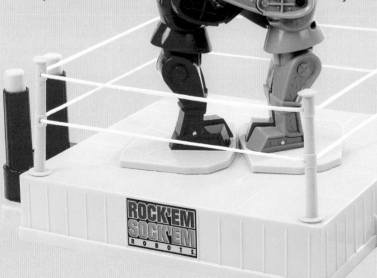

sides controlled how the robots moved around the ring (though that movement was fairly limited) and buttons on the handles let the punches fly. When one robot landed a punch on the other, its head would shoot up and the round would end. It was all kinds of clumsy, but that was part of its charm—that and the unmistakable clash and clatter of the plastic. Sure, there was a modicum of skill involved, but part of the appeal, and what kept kids at it for hours, was that there was enough luck involved that the skill wasn't always the determining factor in winning. It was controlled mayhem, and kids loved it.

In 1977, Marx tried to tap into the success of *Star Wars* and created the Clash of the Cosmic Robots, using that age-old trick: tweak the design and change the colors and—presto!—a new toy is born. However, Clash never really stood a chance in the competitive toy arena of the late 1970s.

Mattel later acquired the rights to the toy, and, inspired by the original robots' brief appearance in *Toy Story 2,* introduced a replica of the original intended for the collector's market in 2000.

A version of the toy is still available, though it's about half the size of the original.

WHERE ARE THEY NOW?

The original toy by Marx was produced into the early 1970s.

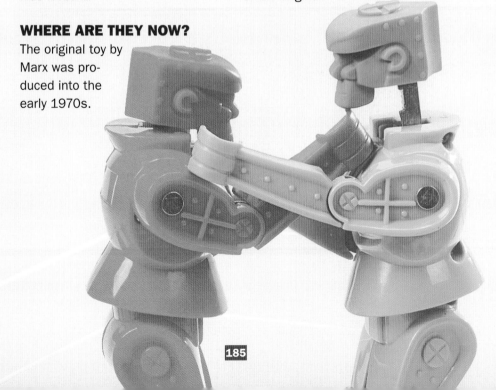

THE TOPPLING TOWER GAME

CAREFUL

Careful

While most games of the 1960s were marketed to little kids, the manufacturers of Careful took a different tack, promoting it as a party game for the new hip generation of teens and adults (a marketing strategy that naturally made it irresistible to younger kids as well).

HOW WE PLAYED IT

Careful made a whole lot of noise and a whole lot of mess. Play centered around a tower that stood almost four feet tall, with four floors built on pillars of red, green, blue, and orange plastic. The object of the game was to remove the pillars without making the tower collapse, which made setting it up almost as strategic and challenging as the game play. Oh, and there was a bell tower on the top that jingled when the tower was at risk of collapsing—which happened pretty often as the game progressed.

On each turn a player would spin the spinner to see which color pillar he or she had to remove. Then came the tricky part: how. You could try to slide the pillar along the maze on each floor level. Or you could try to push it to the middle of a floor and remove it through the hole in the center. Or, if you were really confident, you could lift one floor and pull out the pillar. A truly strategic player might try to rearrange the pillars with each turn to increase his chances of getting his out on the subsequent turn—and perhaps making it more challenging for the next player.

Naturally, this was all to be done amid taunting and heckling from the other players—which would generally reach its zenith when the tower inevitably crashed to the floor. It was certainly one of the largest and loudest games of the period—and often one of the longest; even though the rules suggested that you play as many rounds as you had players, the game often lasted well into the night as tower topplers clamored for one more chance to redeem themselves.

WHERE IS IT NOW?

Careful was only a modest hit, and once the popularity of party games dwindled in the early 1970s, it took a final tumble into obscurity.

But while Careful's sheer size has made it prohibitive to reissue from a cost standpoint, its legacy lives on in Hasbro's Jenga. Jenga's tower may stand only about eighteen inches tall, but the challenge—and the fun—is just as large.

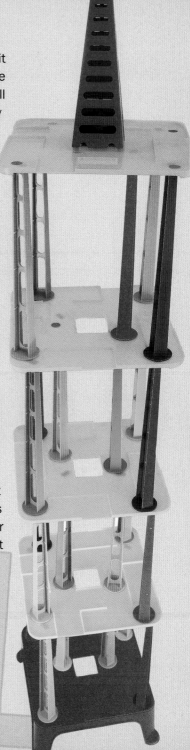

Hands Down 1967

This was a skill-and-action game that required plenty of hand-eye coordination, and skills similar to those required for thumb-wrestling or Slaps (one name for the game where you put your two hands on top of your opponent's and try to move them out of the way before you can be slapped).

HOW WE PLAYED IT

The game was animated by the plastic Slam-O-Matic, a unit that sat in the middle of the table. It had four levers shaped like hands, and each one was connected to a tab in the center. It was essentially a scoring device. When a hand was slapped, its tab descended, so the tab of the last person to slap was plainly and shamefully visible on the top. The idea was not to be the last to slap.

Players were each dealt cards, and took turns drawing from their stacks. If you got a match, you slapped in, and the last person to go Hands Down had to give up a card to the first one. Play continued until one player was out of cards.

Now here was the thing, though: On your turn you could *pretend* to go Hands Down even if you didn't have

a match. Then, the first person to fall for your sleight of hand would have to give up a card, and you might get a match.

WHY WE LOVED IT

It was definitely a fast-paced and noisy game, and fun for groups or parties since you needed at least three people to play.

This was really a basic card game, but the Slam-O-Matic (got to love saying that) added novelty and fun. With its aqua base and funky design it also truly reflected the style sensibilities of its time.

WHERE IS IT NOW?

Poof-Slinky, which currently owns the Ideal brand name, has produced a modern version of the game called Slap Happy. Game play is the same—Slam-O-Matic and all—so new generations can enjoy this classic.

Ker-Plunk 1968

As the onomatopoeic name suggests, the thrill of this game was the moment when all the marbles came crashing down, making that dreaded, but all too familiar, ker-plunking sound.

HOW WE PLAYED IT

Setup was a little tedious. Players threaded long plastic sticks through an octagonal collar around the center of a tube. When all the sticks were in place, marbles were poured into the top of the tube and landed on the crossed sticks, where they precariously balanced. That's when the fun began. On each turn, players removed one stick, and as the number of sticks diminished, the chances of marbles dropping through increased.

Inevitably, one player would pull a stick that would create a cascade of marbles—ker-plunk!—ending the round.

Players often created their own rules to make the game a little more exciting. The one universal rule, though, was that once you touched a stick, you had to remove it.

The game seemed like it had elements of strategy to it, but for the most part, it was really about luck, because as the game progressed, each straw could change the entire setup.

WHY WE LOVED IT

This play pattern—where one wrong move sends everything crashing down—has been part of many different games. Kids love the noise and the mayhem, and moms always liked that the mess was confined to a small space.

Another cool thing about Ker-Plunk was that you could use any marbles, so you could easily replace the ones that inevitably rolled under couches.

WHERE IS IT NOW?

In a testament to the game's timeless appeal, Mattel is still making and selling a version that is slightly smaller than the original.

Uno 1971

One of the reasons that people keep trying to come up with new toys and games is the chance that they'll hit the jackpot. Sure, many—nay, most—fail, but every once in a while a major hit is created. That's what happened with Uno. Developed in 1971 by Merle Robbins, a Cincinnati barber, the game was a variation on many types of basic card games. The object was to get rid of all your cards by playing them one at a time on a card with a matching color or number on the top of the discard pile. Simple? Not so fast.

Robbins put in a lot of twists and turns that kept the game constantly changing, including wild cards, cards that reversed the direction of play, and rules that forced someone on the verge of winning to fill up their hand again. And there's another important rule: When a player has only two cards left and is about to play one, he or she must say "Uno" to warn all the other players that the round is about to end. If the player is caught *not* saying it, he or she has to draw two cards . . . and the hand goes on.

The game is played with a deck of 108 cards—25 cards in four suits with the numbers 0–9. There are also 8 cards that change up the game play. Each player starts with 7 cards, and on each turn must either play or draw.

Part of the appeal of the game was its simplicity. Even with the relatively complex reverses and change-ups that occurred, virtually everything is printed on the cards, so people can just sit down and start playing—an important component of a hit game.

Robbins scraped together $8,000 to produce the first five thousand games and sold them out of his barbershop and other local stores. It was a decent business, but Robbins had never set out to be in the game industry, so in 1972, he sold the rights to the game for $50,000 plus a royalty of 10 cents per game to the newly formed International Games.

As had happened with other games and would with ones in the future (notably Pictionary, in the mid-1980s), grassroots success blossomed into a full-scale hit. With the broader distribution made possible by International Games, more and more people started to play Uno, and it became a minifad by the mid-1970s.

Mattel acquired International Games in 1992, and Uno has become one of the bestselling games of all time.

WHERE IS IT NOW?

Since it's been under the Mattel Games banner, Uno has been produced in hundreds of different versions with themed sets ranging from entertainment to sports. Mattel has introduced a variety of mechanical devices to enhance game play as

well. The game is a bestselling app and a hot computer game, and the annual Uno World Championship in London and Moscow attracts representatives from more than seventy countries.

Dungeons and Dragons
1974

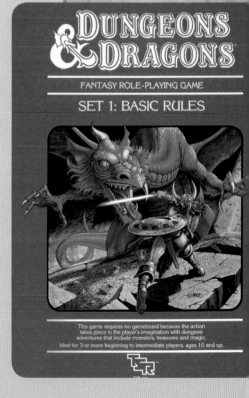

Throughout toy history, the number of toys that have truly transformed the nature of play is relatively few, but Dungeons and Dragons (D&D) is certainly one of them. It introduced an entirely new way to play, drawing new types of players into the world of games and creating an entire subculture surrounding a game.

WHY WE LOVED IT

There had been complex war games before, most of which were sold largely to the military hobbyist audience, but D&D changed the rules entirely. D&D was a *role-playing game,* which meant that instead of mobilizing an army, players actually took on the role of individual characters that they played throughout an adventure. Each game was one story or adventure, and depending on the players, the narratives could get very complex. Each of the players would travel through the world of the story gaining skills, strength, and experience, and engaging in battles, the outcomes of which were determined by the rolls of different dice. Adventures could take hours, days, or even weeks

DUNGEONS & DRAGONS

FANTASY ROLE-PLAYING GAME

SET 1: BASIC RULES

This game requires no gameboard because the action takes place in the player's imagination with dungeon adventures that include monsters, treasures and magic. Ideal for 3 or more beginning to intermediate players, ages 10 and up.

and costumed D&D players soon became the centerpiece of gaming conventions such as Gen Con.

The original game had few parameters, but over the years a more rules-driven game, Advanced Dungeons and Dragons, developed, and the scope of the game kept expanding. Naturally, there were some copycat games, but none would come close to finding such a devoted audience as the original D&D until Magic: The Gathering was introduced in 1993.

to complete, and the game soon amassed a cultlike following across the United States—and the world—particularly in the nerd and geek subcultures, where fantasy worlds had become a refuge from real-life jocks and bullies.

HOW WE PLAYED IT

Each game was overseen by a dungeon master, who dictated the story line and guided the play. Serious dungeon masters would devote hours to developing different adventures, often tailored to the interests of the players. As the game caught on, a secondary market grew around game books, props, and accessories. It wasn't uncommon for kids to dress up as their characters while gaming,

WHERE ARE THEY NOW?

D&D was not free of controversy in its heyday. As the game worked its way into popular culture, it became a target of attacks from religious groups, who likened the game play to Satanism. Soon, urban legends grew up around players who were said to be so distraught over losing they committed suicide. No reported instances of this can actually be found, though it is fair to say that a fair number of D&D players bordered on the obsessed.

D&D continues to be a complete culture among its legions of fans. From events and conventions to new products—both traditional and electronic—the world of D&D is still vibrant, engaged, and nerdy as ever. But in a really good way.

Othello 1975

Although Othello as we know it today was first marketed in the United States in 1975, the game has a long history stretching back to the Victorian era, and it has influenced many similar games, including Reversi, Go, Over-She-Goes, Annex, and others.

Despite the game's roots in the British Empire, it was the Japanese company Tsukuda Original that branded the game with the name Othello. They also created a complex backstory about how the black and white sides of the pieces used in the game represented Shakespeare's Othello and Desdemona, and the green playing board represented the jealousy (Shakespeare's "green-eyed monster") that propelled the plot of the play.

the fact that it was a simple strategy game that had so many possible variations that no two games were ever quite alike. Starting with four checkers in the board, players added a checker with each turn, and if you flanked pieces of the other color, you reversed all of them to your own color. The player with the most of his color once the board filled up was the winner.

The modern version of the game was first introduced in Japan in 1973, and it made its way to American shores when a fan of the game named Jim Becker secured the rights to sell the game in the United States, then licensed them to Gabriel Toys. The game was marketed under a catchy phrase: "A minute to learn. A lifetime to master."

WHY WE LOVED IT

But it wasn't Elizabethan allusions that made the game a hit. It was

WHERE IS IT NOW?

In 1976, Becker arranged the first Othello tournaments, and they've been an annual event ever since, though the winners are not likely to make the evening news as they did in the early 1980s.

With the rise of electronic games and home computers, it's no surprise that many enterprising minds have attempted to computerize the game. The first computer Othello, produced in the early 1980s, was a handheld set the size of a shoebox, and it cost about $100—a staggering sum at the time. Later on, Radica created a handheld version that cost about one-tenth of the original computer version, and it became a small, but dependable, seller.

Othello is still popular worldwide, particularly in Japan, which has produced quite a number of Othello champions. Becker's company reports that more than forty million classic games have been sold in more than one hundred countries.

Hungry Hungry Hippos

1978

One of the best things about classic skill-and-action games is the noise, noise, noise, noise. And Hungry Hungry Hippos delivered on that, and then some. From the first time they set eyes on the marble-eating hippos, kids were hooked on the fast-paced feeding frenzy and the unmistakable clatter of plastic on plastic that is the classic sound track for games of this type.

The game was first created by inventor Fred Kroll in 1967, near the peak of the first frenzy for this type of skill-and-action game that was kicked off by Mouse Trap in 1963. For reasons now lost to history, the game didn't make its debut until more than a decade later when it was first produced by Milton Bradley.

HOW WE PLAYED IT

Four colorful plastic hippos were attached to the four edges of a game board. A bunch of marbles were released

into the center of the board, and then players whacked away on the handles of the hippos, which would stretch their necks so they could gobble up the marbles. The winner was the one who got the most marbles.

But despite what looked like chaos, smart kids knew that there was a strategy to this game; you couldn't just whale away at the levers and hope to win, because when a hippo missed a ball, it could ricochet right into an opponent's mouth. The name of the game was actually *controlled* whacking. Really smart kids also knew to whack differently depending on the number of kids playing because the number of players affected how the marbles would move.

WHERE ARE THEY NOW?

Despite the game's distinctively retro, '70s feel, each new generation of kids has found Hungry Hungry Hippos to be irresistible, and it has never been out of production (though there have been some updates over the years: The marbles are now red instead of white, and some of the hippos have changed colors). There have also been an arcade version and even a travel version that kept all the marbles enclosed in a clear plastic bubble. (Yeah, that's perfect for a long car trip.)

This game may have been loud, boisterous, and annoying to some grown-ups (killjoys), but it was all part of the excitement and silly play that make classic games so popular.

Trivial Pursuit 1982

Wouldn't it be great if the last argument you had with a friend ended up making you both multimillionaires?

Well, that's exactly what happened to Scott Abbott, a sports editor with the Canadian Press, and Chris Haney, photo editor of the *Montreal Gazette*. It started as an argument over who was the better board game player, which turned into a contest to see who had a better grasp of trivial information.

What happened next, though, was anything but trivial. They turned their contest into a board game. At the time, it seemed unlikely that this homespun creation would ever take off. Because its innovative folding board and plastic game pieces (round containers that held six different colored pie-shaped wedges to keep track of correct answers) were expensive to produce, they priced the game at $35, which was astronomical for a game at the time. And as if that wasn't bad enough, the now notoriously difficult trivia questions were clearly aimed toward adults, and conventional wisdom at the time was that

adults didn't play board games. Plus, retailers would never take a square-shaped box that didn't fit into their standard shelf configurations. It was hopeless.

WHY WE LOVED IT

Hopeless at least until people started playing it. For this, Abbott and Haney can thank Linda Pezzano, an innovative marketer with a flair for the nontraditional who they brought in to try to sell adults on a game that tested their knowledge of often-arcane information. Pezzano sent games to every celebrity

mentioned in the game, hosted parties for the media at her house, and gave away sample game cards to just about anyone who would look at them. The tactics worked. Over the next year, this tsunami of publicity made Trivial Pursuit a must-have item in millions of households. At a time when game manufacturers considered selling one hundred thousand units of a game to be a success, Trivial Pursuit was selling millions. In fact, between 1983 and 1985, more than thirty million sets were produced. Its popularity attracted lawsuits, saying Abbott and Haney had stolen the questions or the very idea of the game, but the courts consistently ruled in favor of the creators.

The debut of Trivial Pursuit was a game-changing event. Thanks to Pezzano's smart PR efforts, adults across the country were suddenly throwing parties just as an excuse to play the game, introducing the tradition of "game night"—something that hadn't previously existed—that would become a fixture of adult social life for the next thirty-plus years.

WHERE IS IT NOW?

Not surprisingly, the success of Trivial Pursuit ushered in a boom in trivia games: everything from Bible trivia to music trivia to sports trivia and virtually any other topic you could think of. None of the spin-offs had the longevity of Trivial Pursuit, which by then had emerged as a bona fide brand; by the twentieth anniversary of the game, Milton Bradley estimated that it had sold more than seventy million copies in seventeen countries and twenty-six languages.

Today, Hasbro makes about fifteen different versions of the game—including collector's editions and specialized editions, including a sports edition and a book lover's edition—most of which are updated every few years to stay current. The game has had online versions, been on TV, and even inspired a Vegas slot machine. Jackpot, indeed.

Not a bad way to settle a score between friends, is it?

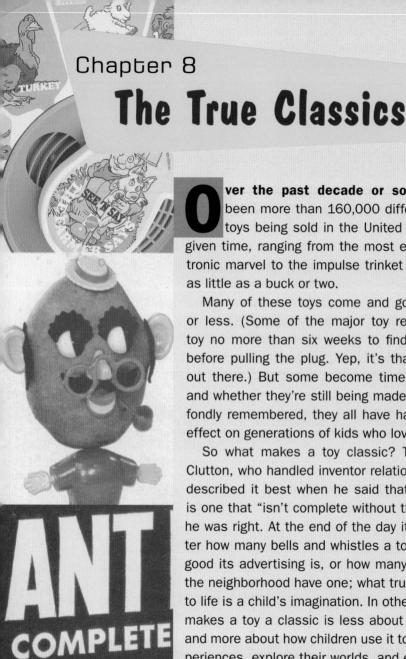

Chapter 8

The True Classics

Over the past decade or so, there have been more than 160,000 different types of toys being sold in the United States at any given time, ranging from the most elaborate electronic marvel to the impulse trinket that can cost as little as a buck or two.

Many of these toys come and go in a season or less. (Some of the major toy retailers give a toy no more than six weeks to find an audience before pulling the plug. Yep, it's that competitive out there.) But some become timeless classics, and whether they're still being made or are simply fondly remembered, they all have had a profound effect on generations of kids who loved them.

So what makes a toy classic? The late Stan Clutton, who handled inventor relations for Mattel, described it best when he said that the best toy is one that "isn't complete without the child." And he was right. At the end of the day it doesn't matter how many bells and whistles a toy has, or how good its advertising is, or how many other kids in the neighborhood have one; what truly brings a toy to life is a child's imagination. In other words, what makes a toy a classic is less about the toy itself, and more about how children use it to have new experiences, explore their worlds, and express themselves. Indeed, it is the sense of self-exploration that makes a play experience truly memorable.

Classic play falls into three big categories: physical play, social play, and solo play. Each of these is important to the emotional and cognitive development of a child. You may not have thought about it, but when preschoolers repeat the letters of the alphabet, they are building a structure for acquiring language. When they learn to be good losers or good winners of board games, they're learning how to keep the triumphs and tragedies of life in perspective. And when they build with bricks, they are developing the skills and creativity to solve problems and imagine solutions.

But whether they build character or not, what makes these classic toys so dear to our hearts is simply all the fun we had—and that's a great thing. In all those years we spent dreading school, avoiding our homework, and eagerly seeking the release of playtime, we never knew that our toys and games were building the foundation of who we would be today. But they were, and thank goodness for that, because amid all of the responsibilities, challenges, and harsh realities we face in our adult lives, there's nothing better than occasionally pausing to unleash our inner child by recalling the magic of the classic toys we played with.

LEGO (1932; arrived in the United States in 1961)

While the Group was formed in 1932, it wasn't until the early 1960s that LEGO became a household name worldwide. In the 1930s, the Billund, Denmark–based maker of wooden home products started to focus more on making toys. Its name is an abbreviation of *leg godt,* Danish for "play well." Only later did founder Ole Kirk Christiansen realize that *lego* in Latin means "I study" or "I put together."

In 1947, the company began making injection-molded plastic toys, including a line called Automatic Binding Bricks. Over the next eight years, the company developed and perfected these bricks, renamed them LEGO bricks, and expanded distribution into Germany.

WHY WE LOVED THEM

In 1958, LEGO introduced the iconic interlocking design and construction system. Now kids could build even bigger and more complex models because the locking bricks were more stable and made structures difficult to topple. So while there had been plenty of building sets before—even brick-based ones, such as American Bricks, which were for a time manufactured by Elgo Plastics—what set LEGO apart was how well their bricks held together and the whole new world of creativity and imagination this opened up.

Few people know how LEGO toys got to the United States. They arrived, almost literally, in a suitcase. In the late 1950s, the then-president of Samsonite luggage was visiting Belgium. He came across a LEGO set in a toy store and was instantly intrigued. So he went to Denmark and tracked the company down.

Luckily, LEGO executives had thought about expanding into the United States for awhile, so when Samsonite offered to devote part of its factory in Loveland, Colorado, to creating LEGO bricks, they jumped on board. (Samsonite was known for its hard plastic suitcases at the time, which were also made with injection molding.)

Knowing that architects such as Eero Saarinen had been using LEGO bricks to build architectural models, Samsonite's young publicist Barry Schwartz took the bricks to the Pratt Institute, where he convinced aspiring architects to use them to build models of a city of the future. This got the attention of producers of the *Today* show.

Another early adopter was Norman Mailer. One day Schwartz received a call from the author, who simply wanted to build something

using the sturdy, colorful blocks. So Schwartz had the company send the thousands of pieces Mailer had requested, and six months later, Schwartz recalled, "We went to his house, and there's was an incredible 'Rube Goldberg-ish' thing made of LEGO." The media loved it, and LEGO was on its way.

But the LEGO Group was still struggling to get the attention of *toy buyers*. So Schwartz convinced the company to set up a booth in the Danish Pavilion at the 1964–65 New York World's Fair, where parents could leave their children to build and play while they explored the grounds.

WHERE ARE THEY NOW?

LEGO bricks are one of the few toys that have stayed exactly the same over the years (the company understands the importance of sticking with what works). The design of the bricks has never changed, and many a set have been handed down from parents to kids—that is, if the parents will give them up. Few toys have inspired as many active adult collectors and players as LEGO over the years.

As popular as the bricks were (and are), it was not always smooth sailing for the LEGO Group. Despite getting the *Star Wars* license in 1998—a huge coup for sales—by the middle of the first decade of the twenty-first century, the company was having financial trouble. It all began when the patent on its stud-and-tube coupling system expired. Competitors rushed in to the market, and LEGO spent years in litigation, losing in every country.

But sometimes adversity can spur creativity, and today LEGO is more successful than ever. Even with direct competition in the block market from a number of manufacturers, LEGO is posting record growth.

The company has expanded its *Star Wars* line as well as other licenses, and reinvigorated its Technic, Hero Factory, and LEGO City building sets. And it's made itself more relevant for the twenty-first century by expanding into theme parks and robotics, including the wildly successful Mindstorms line

and a play lab at the Massachusetts Institute of Technology.

But perhaps the most dramatic area of growth has been in gaming and narrative-based play, including its popular Ninjago line of characters and stories introduced in 2011. The company has expanded into online play and video games, creating a more dynamic and contemporary play experience. In 2012, LEGO finally introduced LEGO Friends, a line aimed primarily at the way girls traditionally play. Still, the appeal of LEGO all goes back to the building, and today's kids and adults love that as much as ever.

DID YOU KNOW?
Gladys Knight and the Pips were huge LEGO fans, and one of the Pips' daughters once won a LEGO building competition—and a trip to Billund, Denmark.

View-Master 1940

While the View-Master was first introduced at the 1939–40 New York World's Fair, like so many other toys, it had long roots in the culture. In the 1850s, the Stereopticon, which allowed people to view 3-D pictures of exotic locations, became a sensation on both sides of the Atlantic. At the time, this was considered exciting home entertainment.

Nearly a century later, William Gruber came up with the idea of putting color movie film inside a handheld viewing device with two eyepieces, when he discovered that two photos taken from slightly different perspectives and laid over each other created the 3-D effect when viewed through the binocular lenses. So Gruber put ten of these images on a disc that fit into his viewer and could be advanced by pushing down on a lever.

Not originally intended as a toy, the View-Master went the postcard one better and brought locations such as the Grand Canyon, Venice, and Carlsbad Caverns to life. Gru-

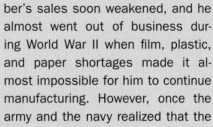

ber's sales soon weakened, and he almost went out of business during World War II when film, plastic, and paper shortages made it almost impossible for him to continue manufacturing. However, once the army and the navy realized that the View-Master could be used in training, they ordered one hundred thousand viewers and six million reels, saving Gruber's company.

In the 1950s, as TV and other entertainment for kids took off, the View-Master started to become a kids' toy.

WHERE IS IT NOW?

Over the years, many different versions of the View-Master were introduced, though boomers will most likely remember the brown Bakelite unit that was introduced in 1955 and stayed in production for the next fifteen years.

The View-Master is still sold today, marketed primarily to parents of preschoolers. As technology has become more sophisticated, and 3-D movies and television shows have become commonplace, today's kids aren't impressed by images that would have wowed viewers nearly seventy years ago.

Magic 8 Ball 1950

Every civilization and every era has had its favorite ways of telling the future. In fifteenth-century Italy, tarot cards made their first appearance. In the Victorian age, seers marketed crude gizmos and gadgets designed to help those beclouded in the mortal sphere determine their destinies by communing with the spirit world. In 1892, in the United States, this fascination went mass-market with the introduction of the Ouija board. And who could forget the timeless crystal ball? Consumers have never been able to get enough of any product that promises to provide a peek into the world of the unknown.

While many versions of the Magic 8 Ball had been developed and patented over several years starting in the mid-1940s, the classic version we all know and love wasn't produced on a large scale until 1950. Alabe Crafts called it the Magic 8 Ball, ostensibly because to be "behind the 8 ball" was popular slang for being in a pickle—or a disadvantageous position on the pool table—though there are other stories about the name's origin. However the name came about, this plastic prognosticator had the answer for any question you could pose to it, though it was marketed "for entertainment purposes only."

WHY WE LOVED IT

Like any good fortune-telling device, the Magic 8 Ball is simple to operate. Ask it a question. Give it a shake and turn it over and in a few moments the answer will float into view in the window in the base of the ball. The "Spirit Slate," as that floating fortune teller was called, is a hollow icosahedron (that's twenty sides) with text printed on each side that somehow remains readable through the inky liquid that fills the ball.

The Magic 8 Ball's answers are often noncommittal and, like those of any swami worthy of a palm crossed with silver, open to interpretation: "Signs Point to Yes," "Outlook Not So Good," "My Reply Is No" or, a favorite, "Better Not Tell You Now," You might want to think twice before making stock picks on the advice of the Magic 8 Ball.

WHERE IS IT NOW?

Today the original Magic 8 Ball is a kitsch icon, and Mattel has produced timely tie-ins over the years, ranging from Harry Potter to Sponge-Bob SquarePants, as well as various parody versions.

While foretelling the future is always an imperfect art, I predict the Magic 8 Ball will continue to be a favorite for many more years to come.

Ask a Question...
Turn Over for the Answer!

TRY ME!

Ages 6 and up

MAGIC 8 BALL

MOST LIKELY

SIGNS POINT TO YES

ASK AGAIN LATER

The Magic 8 Ball Has All the Answers. Look on the Back!

MAGIC 8 BALL

30188

Ages 6 and up

Little People 1950

I n Hollywood, even the biggest stars have to start out playing small parts. This was the case for Fisher-Price's Little People, who got their start playing the role of the tiny firemen who manned Fisher-Price's 1950 toy Looky Fire Truck. Over the rest of the decade, these bit players began to take on bigger and bigger parts, giving wooden, but imagination-filled, performances on a stagecoach, a sports car, and later,

famously, on the all-time Little People favorite: the school bus.

Throughout the 1960s, the peg characters began to appear in all kinds of play sets—including a train, a farm, and an amusement park. In 1975, they even found sunny days on *Sesame Street*. Soon they gained such celebrity that they began to be sold separately under the name Play Family.

In 1985, the Play Family was re-

named Little People, though they still retained their peglike look. It wasn't until 1997 that the characters became more peoplelike, with arms, legs, and actual faces. Today, the five leading characters all have names—Eddie, Maggie, Sonya Lee, Michael, and Sarah Lynn.

WHY WE LOVED THEM

The evolution of the Little People from abstract, faceless pegs attached as an afterthought to a toy fire truck, to humanlike, fully developed characters with their own story lines, reflects the changing nature of play over the past half century. This shift has been driven by advances in toy making, the ubiquity of television, the importance of story and narrative surrounding toy lines, and children's deepening attachment to their toys.

WHERE ARE THEY NOW?

The Little People's star still shines, and in recent years, they have been featured in videos, apps, and much more.

Still, in the case of the Little People, kids' imaginations have always been the real star of the show—and that's a very big part of the fun.

Silly Putty 1950

World War II had a profound impact on the toy industry, at least indirectly. Thanks to wartime rationing and the scarcity of materials used for weapons or warfare, chemists around the country worked hard to develop synthetic alternatives to use in manufacturing. One desperately needed item was synthetic rubber. To that end, in 1943 a Scottish-born engineer named James Wright, who was working in the General Electric labs, combined boric acid and silicone oil and created a polymer that bounced when dropped on the floor. For the next six years, General Electric tried to find practical applications for the putty, to no avail.

WHY WE LOVED IT

The bouncing putty may not have been particularly useful, but it was fun—at least that's what Ruth Fallgatter, owner of a New Haven, Connecticut, toy store thought. In fact, she liked it so much she decided to sell it in her catalog. It did well, but not as well as Fallgatter had expected, so she sold the rights to marketing consultant Peter Hodgson.

Hodgson renamed the product Silly Putty, and, as it was Easter time, began packaging one-ounce blobs of the stuff in plastic eggs (they were readily available, cheap, and held the right amount of putty) and shipping them in surplus egg boxes.

But the Silly Putty fad didn't truly hatch until August 1950, when a write-up about the oddly packaged plaything appeared in the *New Yorker*'s "Talk of the Town" section. Within three days, Hodgson had orders for more than 250,000 pieces. This was great PR, but, as had happened before and would happen again, it was TV advertising that really put the putty over the top. After all, on a commercial, kids could see how much fun it was to bounce, stretch, and even pick up newsprint on the putty—then ball it up and start all over again.

WHERE IS IT NOW?

In the ensuing years, Silly Putty would go to the moon and travel the world. In the 1980s, it became a retro classic; baby boomers were more than happy to shell out a few dollars for the fun of sharing this timeless classic—available in most toy and drugstores—with their own kids.

It also has a bunch of handy household uses. For instance, Silly Putty won't damage most contact lenses, so if you lose a contact, you may find it by gently rolling the putty around where you think you dropped it. If you don't find the lens, you can always use the putty to relieve the stress of losing it.

NOT-SO-FUN FACT:
If you've tried to pick up your favorite newsprint lately, you might have been disappointed. The Silly Putty is the same as it always was, but newspapers have changed. When Silly Putty first came out, oil-based inks on newsprint stayed on the surface of the paper. Newer inks absorb into it. But you can still pick up pencil marks, if that's any consolation.

DID YOU KNOW?

Mr. Potato Head was the first major mass-market toy ever advertised on TV. The success of this advertising program transformed how toys were marketed, as toy companies realized that children's requests would soon wield great influence over their parents' pocketbooks.

ONION

CUCUMBER

PEAR

Mr. Potato Head 1952

Many hit toys have one thing in common: They allow kids to break the rules in a way that's fun and often parent approved. In 1952, Mr. Potato Head came along to let kids shatter Mom's cardinal admonition "Don't play with your food."

WHY WE LOVED HIM

Mr. Potato Head was never meant to be a toy—at least not in the traditional sense. Designer George Lerner intended the body parts to be the kind of cheap trinkets kids could delight in finding at the bottom of a cereal box. The breakfast cereal would provide the hands, eyes, noses, and pipe, but the kids would be responsible for producing the head—the potato.

Hasbro, however, had other ideas. A couple of cheap plastic body parts didn't seem like much of a toy, so Hasbro decided they would provide the potato. Problem was, the original potato head was made of Styrofoam and couldn't hold up to the endless facial rearrangements that were the basis of the play. Creative kids quickly turned to the vegetable crisper, and those who played with

the original will remember how mom got tired of reaching for the produce and finding it full of little holes. Hasbro responded with a virtual vegetable frenzy, for a brief time marketing orange, pepper, cucumber, and carrot heads before reverting back to the classic potato.

Owners of the original Mr. Potato Head may remember that the top of the body used to be outfitted with a sharp spike—all the better for impaling the potato. The other pieces had sharp points and edges as well, which made them easier to stick into the potatoes but put kids at risk for collateral damage. In 1964, Hasbro introduced a round, plastic, hazardless potato and has sold millions and millions since.

WHERE IS HE NOW?

As the baby boomers aged, Mr. Potato Head transitioned from plaything to pop culture icon. His simple yet unmistakable appearance made him a slam-dunk for publicity stunts, and Hasbro took full advantage. In 1984, Mr. Potato Head ran for mayor of Boise, Idaho. (He didn't win.) And in the late 1980s, he gave up his

iconic pipe as part of the Great American Smokeout with Surgeon General C. Everett Koop.

But his big Hollywood break came in 1995 when the character of Mr. Potato Head, voiced by Don Rickles, delighted viewers in the movie *Toy Story*. For baby boomers, now approaching or in their fifties (and likely viewing the movie with their grandchildren), the role of the endearing curmudgeon with a wry sense of humor was the ultimate encore for their beloved tuber.

Today, Mr. Potato Head is as much known for being a vehicle for parody than anything else. He's been outfitted for different professional teams, appeared as "Spider-Spud" (a spoof of Spider-Man), and, perhaps most famously, "Darth Tater," the perfect mash-up of two baby boomer darlings—*Star Wars* and Mr. Potato Head.

As of 2012, more than one hundred million Mr. and Mrs. Potato Head toys have been sold. He has become a Spud for All Seasons.

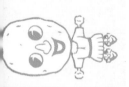

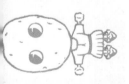

Gumby 1955

While certainly a cultural icon immediately recognizable to three generations of toy lovers, Gumby is known mostly for his innocent expression and his long, stretchy arms. What many people don't know is that he was never meant to be a toy at all. He was conceived by illustrator Art Clokey as a character for an animated jazz video, but studio heads thought he was more appropriate for a children's movie, so they tasked Clokey to experiment with an emerging animation style called stop-motion. After creating a number of more abstract clay figures, Clokey finally hit on Gumby.

WHY WE LOVED HIM

The design of Gumby was eminently practical, aesthetically speaking. For stop-motion animation—which involves changing the position of an object in tiny increments over a sequence of individually photographed frames, creating the appearance of movement when the frames are played one after the other—the figure needed to be easy to pose, again and again.

Gumby's body was inspired by the fairy-tale character the Gingerbread Man, and his head by an old photograph of Clokey's father. Why green? Easy. Clokey liked green. In all,

Clokey thought he was funny looking and believed children would as well. He was right.

In 1957, *The Gumby Show* premiered, a kids' program featuring live action and a variety of shorts (all created by Clokey) starring Gumby; his horse pal, Pokey; Nopey the dog; and the evil Blockheads. Though the series was never a breakout hit, the innocence of Gumby and the way he always got out of jams made him a sympathetic and appealing character to kids, and he was popular enough to inspire toys, which were made with flexible plastic stretched over wire frames so kids could bend them and re-create the story lines of the shorts.

WHERE IS HE NOW?

Gumby might have languished in obscurity were it not for two events. The first was a resurgence of interest in the original shorts in the 1980s; they were seen as "retro" and therefore cool. This led to a new series of programs in which Gumby led, of all things, a rock band.

But the person Gumby really has to thank for his '80s renaissance is Eddie Murphy, who played Gumby in a variety of skits on *Saturday Night Live,* starting in 1982. Murphy popularized the phrase "I'm Gumby, damn it," and portrayed Gumby as a *seemingly* sweet character who turned into an abusive curmudgeon as soon as the cameras weren't rolling. The spoofs gave the affable Gumby the one thing he'd apparently been missing: an edge. People loved the skits, and they instantly sparked a new interest in the toys, largely among the older set. Today, Gumby is more than classic: He's kitsch, which is why you can mostly find him in stores that deal in retro toys targeted to consumers age thirty and over. And even there you'll probably find only Gumby and Pokey. Nopey, Prickle (a dinosaur), and the Blockheads are nowhere to be found.

Uncle Milton's Ant Farm

1956

When you get right down to it, doesn't every kid have a fascination with bugs? Certainly Milton Levine did, as he watched kids playing with an anthill in the early 1950s and, as the company legend goes, recalled his own juvenile ant collection.

Kids had pets of all kinds—from goldfish to dogs and cats—but

these were just single pets. What if they could have an entire world within their view?

That was the idea behind the original ant farm. It was a narrow plastic unit with clear sides and sand in it. In 1956, kids bought the farm for $1.29, and sent away for the ants, which arrived a couple of weeks later in the mail.

TV advertising helped make the ant farm a huge hit, and the company heavily promoted the fact that the ant farm was unbreakable and escape proof. Many baby boomers recall that maternal fear of a house overrun by ants was the biggest obstacle to their getting one. But some

See the ANTS . . .
BUILDING BRIDGES
DIGGING SUBWAYS
MOVING MOUNTAINS

Ants

ts today. They ca

nia on the map.

they

a   about 20

a de

ed

moms believed that the scientific value outweighed the infestation threat, and in the late 1950s, Uncle Milton was shipping thousands of ant farms (formally known as "antariums") every week. Incidentally, Mom shouldn't have worried. Uncle Milton has always used male harvester ants and has always said that it's illegal to send queen ants, so even if they could escape, the ants couldn't reproduce.

WHY WE LOVED THEM

The ant farm gave kids a glimpse into an unseen world in a way no book or documentary could. They could watch in wonder and observe how the tunnels were made, how the ants were largely nocturnal, and how they did things like bury their dead. It was nature, right in your own bedroom.

WHERE ARE THEY NOW?

The ant farm has never been out of production. In recent years, Uncle Milton has introduced different varieties of the farm, including one using a gel that provides both food and water to the ants, making it much easier to care for them. In 2010, the company introduced the Ant Farm Revolution, a cylindrical ant farm with a light inside that projects large images of the ants on the ceiling. Despite these upgrades, the original classic version is still available.

DID YOU KNOW?
The ants lived only several weeks, depending on how well the kids took care of them. And then they got to watch the ants bury their dead. Fun!

UNBREAKABLE • ESCAPEPROOF •

FASCINATING

ANT FARM

COMPLETE WITH ANTS

See the ANTS . . .
BUILDING BRIDGES
DIGGING SUBWAYS
MOVING MOUNTAINS

Show'N Tell c.1957

In the late 1950s, the filmstrip was considered a breakthrough for educators—and great entertainment for students. Static pictures were projected on a screen, while an accompanying vinyl record provided the sound. (It would beep when the frame was supposed to be advanced.) Children of the '60s will recall watching countless filmstrips—about everything from the history of the universe to how babies are born—in school. Virtually every teacher used them, and for kids they were an exciting break from normal classroom activities.

WHY WE LOVED IT
General Electric introduced the Show'N Tell as a way for kids to enjoy filmstrips—and a real record player—at home. The unit looked like a small TV with a turntable on top. Filmstrips were slid into a slot and the images were projected on the screen while a record played the story; the filmstrip even advanced automatically. Pure magic.

To go with the players, GE produced Picturesound movies that ran just about four minutes—as long as a seven-inch, $33^1/_3$ RPM record could play.

Naturally, this called for some severe editing when it came to adapting literary classics. For instance, in *The Wizard of Oz,* Dorothy had all of four minutes to meet all her friends, visit Oz, defeat the Wicked Witch, and beam herself back at home. There were similar treatments of *Gulliver's Travels, The Swiss Family Robinson,* fairy tales, and the classic Disney movies, as well as science and other educational topics.

Kids loved the toy and found the radically abridged stories engaging and hilarious. While it seemed magical to them, the mechanism was very simple. The eight-inch-long filmstrips sat in a plastic frame that slid into the machine and had teeth along one side. When the filmstrip was inserted in the viewer, the teeth engaged with a sprocket that turned after every seven rotations of the turntable, raising the filmstrip and advancing to the next image. Synching wasn't exact, and kids had to manually turn the turntable a couple of times to get the sound and pictures to start correctly, but kids loved that they could work it themselves, and by the mid-1960s, hundreds of titles had been produced.

WHERE IS IT NOW?

By the mid-1960s, the Show'N Tell seemed archaic, and General Electric stopped making it.

However, in the early 1980s, the Child Guidance brand (a division of CBS Toys) revived the player, naming it a Phono-Viewer. It used the same records and filmstrips, but it

could also project on the wall. New programs were created featuring *Sesame Street,* Disney, and other properties, as well as some original programs.

It's retro appeal was enough to spur a short revival, but it quickly faded away.

In today's world, where movies can be downloaded in moments, the Show'N Tell is a relic of another time, fondly remembered by some, but forgotten by others.

16

33

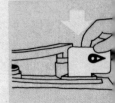

SHOW'N TELL*
picturesound® program

*Trademark General Electric Company 1969, © General Electric Company 1969

Sit 'n Spin 1974

Really, what is it about spinning that is so exciting to kids? Maybe it's the thrill of being able to whirl around in ways that make adults queasy. Or maybe they just love the way the world seems to whiz past them as they spin. That's certainly the appeal of playground merry-go-rounds and amusement park rides.

The toy maker Kenner was certainly aware of the popularity of playground rides when, in 1974, they introduced the Sit 'n Spin. Now kids could have dizzy fun at home anytime. The toy was very simple. One large disk sat firmly on the floor and had a steering column attached to it; a second, concentric disk sat on top of that and spun freely. Kids sat on the upper disk, crossed their legs around the steering column, and pulled on the wheel on the top of the steering column to get themselves spinning.

WHERE IS IT NOW?

Over the years, the toy has remained basically unchanged, though it's been updated to feature different characters. Today it's still readily available from Playskool—and probably will be for generations to come.

Give-A-Show Projector 1959

It wasn't much more than a flashlight with a holder for filmstrips on the front, but at the time it garnered the kind of excitement that company of Huckleberry Hound, Mr. Magoo, Yogi Bear, Popeye, Bozo, Atom Ant, Secret Squirrel, Clyde Crashcup, and many more any time

announcements of the latest iPhone do today. Back when kids could see their favorite cartoon shows only once a week, what was better than being able to enjoy the

color TV was a novelty, and TV shows for kids were either on early mornings or weekends. The novelty of the Give-A-Show Projector was that it put kids in charge of their own entertainment.

Plus, adults who remember this toy from their childhood will recall, in addition to the thrill of having their own projector and being able to run the show, how much fun it was to distort the picture on the walls and ceilings, simply by moving the projector.

they wanted? There was nary a popular cartoon show or sitcom during the period that didn't have a Give-A-Show slide strip to accompany it.

WHY WE LOVED IT

The toy included the projector and a bunch of slides, and kids could project them on any wall or the ceiling. It was pretty low-tech, but kids didn't mind. In the early 1960s, home slideshows were all the rage, and this was a kids' version of the home movies they saw their parents screening at dinner parties. It's easy to forget that when the Give-A-Show Projector first hit the shelves,

WHERE IS IT NOW?

As one might expect, home video and cable TV quickly finished off the Give-A-Show Projector. As the VCR became standard in homes and as favorite cartoons were seen five days a week or more in syndication, kids had a new level of access to entertainment and little need for the Give-A-Show Projector.

Every once in a while, you'll find one of these in an antiques store, but aside from a few blogs and collector's sites, this toy is a relic of another time.

Thimble City 1964

If you never had one, it might be hard to imagine the appeal of Thimble City and the hours of play it inspired. It wasn't much more than a piece of beaverboard with plastic legs, forming a stage of sorts, and some cutout buildings, but Remco's Thimble City had as close to a cult following as a toy could have in the early 1960s.

The toy was like a stage set: a street scene with a fire station, supermarket, service station, and some other stores and office buildings. But what brought Thimble City to life were the magnetic wands that kids placed under the base to move the cars and small figures around the miniature city.

The magnets on the wands would connect to magnets on the underside of the vehicles and figures, so it looked like they were moving on their own around the Thimble City world. Using the wands, kids could park cars in parking spaces, drive through the car wash, and move people up and down the street and even through the swinging doors of the various buildings.

WHY WE LOVED IT
This was open-ended, imaginative play at its best. The magnets may have been the "magic" that animated the cars and people, but it was truly the magic of kids' imaginations that gave life to the city.

The toy was so successful that in 1965 Remco introduced Thimble

REMCO

🔟

Thimble City

7.92

City Union Station. It worked exactly the same way, but instead of a quiet city, kids created the bustling world of a train station.

Union Station soon eclipsed Thimble City in popularity, largely because of its catchy TV commercial. Adults who were kids at the time can still quote today: "Thimble City Union Station. Railroad center of the nation."

WHERE IS IT NOW?

Like any popular toy, these had their day and disappeared after a couple of years, especially as toys emerged that put the emphasis more on speed and competition than on quotidian life in a miniature town.

Today, these are rare to find, even for collectors, and nearly fifty years later, Thimble City exists mostly as a memory—and a fragment of a commercial jingle—for those who once brought its streets to life.

See 'N Say 1965

You can count on it: When a feature proves successful in one kind of toy, manufacturers scramble to put it into others. Sure enough, the incredible success of Chatty Cathy prompted toy makers to try to find ways to use the pull-string-activated talking unit in other toys.

Though by 1965 there had been a number of different talking toys, none were strictly educational toys, which until then had been limited to no-frills affairs such as flash cards, magnetic letters, and puzzles. Mattel saw the opportunity to revolutionize educational toys by adding technology to make them talk.

WHY WE LOVED IT

See 'N Say worked very much like the name suggested. The child pointed the plastic arrow in the center of the round unit to the picture of the animal he or she wanted to hear and pulled the string. The arrow would then spin around, which would engage a needle, which would project the vibrations through a plastic cone, just like on a gramophone, at which point kids would be treated to the sounds of their animal of choice—ducks, dogs, frogs, or the cow with a long, rumbly "Moo-oo-oo." Pulling the string as it was winding back into the unit sometimes caused it to stutter, which to some kids was the height of humor.

Parents loved it because it was educational—especially after Mattel introduced versions with even more traditional learning subjects, such as numbers and letters. The toy also proved to be very durable; it could survive just about any drop or sibling attack.

WHERE IS IT NOW?

Today the See 'N Say is as popular as ever, even in a world powered by tablets and smartphones. Fisher-Price currently makes about ten different models, and not surprisingly, there have been versions featuring Snoopy, Dora the Explorer, and other characters. Though the technology has been brought up to date—the pull string was replaced by a lever, and later the playback device was replaced by a computer chip—the cows still go moo and the ducks still go quack, and the basic look and play have never changed.

Weebles 1971

Whether you played with them or not, you can probably quote the tagline: "Weebles wobble, but they don't fall down." That was the charm and the fun of these egg-shaped toys. According to Hasbro's history, the toys were inspired by the popular "bop bags," punching bags that had weighted bottoms that would stand back up after kids punched them down. Weebles were miniature versions of those—without the punching.

WHY WE LOVED THEM

Kids loved playing with the Weebles and wobbling them, and loved that they had their pick of a wide variety of play sets. There were farms, amusement parks, a circus, and others. There were also accessories that kept the Weebles stationary while kids played with them. If a kid could do it, the logic went, a Weeble could, too, and there were all kinds of activities, such as riding in cars and boats, swinging on swings, and more.

All of the play revolved around the fact that at some point the Weeble would stop wobbling and come to a rest, and then the kids would knock them back into action. (For a one-year-old, this is comedy.)

As the line grew, other innovations, including a glow-in-the-dark Weeble, emerged, and kids began collecting them. Special holiday versions were created, as were Disney and *Sesame Street* sets.

WHERE ARE THEY NOW?

Weebles disappeared in the 1990s, but in the early 2000s, Hasbro's

Playskool brand reintroduced them, and they've been a staple ever since. For a while, Playskool introduced Weebles that were more doll-like, but those didn't do well, and they returned to the eggs.

Modern Weebles are a lot larger than the originals, and like many other classics there is a strong collector community for the toys. Terry Hoknes has written a book, *The Complete Weebles Toy Index, History and Price Guide 1971–2011,* for those who really want to dig deeply into their world.

ACKNOWLEDGMENTS

In what I do, I've talked to thousands of people about their toys. Few things make a face light up like the memory of a favorite plaything, and I've had the privilege to hear so many stories—both heartwarming and hilarious—and am grateful to everyone who has shared those with me.

This book would not have come together without the enthusiasm and expertise of a lot of people. Maryann Karinch is a sweet and savvy agent who saw the possibility of a book in an errant pun. How rare a talent is that? Talia Krohn of Crown Publishers is a dream editor whose willingness to play, and warm, personal support contributed so much to this effort. Production editor Tricia Wygal and copy editor Michelle Daniel kept me on track, and no detail was too small for their keen attention. And, of course, thanks to designer Lauren Dong as well as to everyone at Crown who got into the lighthearted spirit of this book.

I am also incredibly grateful to Marisa Train for the amazing new photography. Her spirit and creativity was a complete joy.

And then there's the support, help and interest of all my colleagues in the toy industry. I couldn't possibly name them all here, and I'm grateful for them every day. They are the ones creating lasting play for today's kids. Among them, though, I owe heartfelt thanks to Michele Litzky, a colleague and dear friend for 30 years; Jim Silver, Bob Glaser and Andy Krinner, my partners at TimetoPlayMag.com, and our whole incredible team; Jeff McKinney, who works with me every day and keeps me laughing—and who kept his *Star Wars* and Transformers figures; Ira Gallen, whose memories are almost as whacked as mine—and who had an original Mystery Date; Neil and Amanda Friedman; and Barry Schwartz for his memories—and for teaching me the toy business when I was just starting out.

I'm grateful to people who helped me track down toys and images; Sara Rosales, Rachel Cooper, Jale Lowery and everyone at Mattel who supported this effort; Julie Duffy and the team at Hasbro; Josslynne Welch, Kaylie Nelson and the Litzky PR team; Bob Pagano and Ron Cohen at Kids Only; Dennis Clausen at Wham-O; Ross Albert of the Albert Design Company; Tim Kimber and Virginia Merritt at PlaSmart; Amanda Santoro at LEGO; Hillary Fine at Uncle Milton; Martin Killgallon at Ohio Art and Paul Reinoehl for the pictures of Big Loo and King Zor.

I also have to thank my brothers, Richard, Bob and Larry, with whom I shared many toys and even if they could turn a game of Risk into a contact sport or try to swipe my Matchbox cars. Thanks, too, to the friends who have given me such unflagging support over many years: Linda Kraus D'Isa, Ashley Rogers, Frank Coker, Linda Verdon, Jennifer Deare, Beth Greenberg, Rick & Addie McCabe, Steve & Christine Sullivan, Ginny Gotides, Ellen Baker, David Kozinski and Patti Mengers Kozinski.

And finally, thanks to all my teachers at the Tower Hill School—despite the fact that they took away my toys, put me in detention and warned me that too much play would lead to no good.

ILLUSTRATION CREDITS

Air Blaster, pages 3, 7, 9, 134, 135: WHAM-O® Air Blaster is a registered trademark of Wham-O. Photo ©2013 Wham-O. All rights reserved.

Ant Farm, pages 202, 221, 222, 223: Ant Farm® is a registered trademark of Uncle Milton, Inc. ©2013 Uncle Milton, Inc. All rights reserved. Photos used with permission.

Baby Alive, pages 28, 29: © 2013 Hasbro, Inc. Used with permission.

Barbie, pages 17, 18, 19: © 2013 Mattel, Inc. Barbie® is a registered trademark of Mattel, Inc.

Beautiful Crissy, pages 14, 26, 27: photo by Marisa Train, © 2013 Christopher Byrne.

Big Loo, pages 67, 72, 73: photo ©2013 Paul Reinhol. All rights reserved. Used with permission.

Big Wheel, pages 11, 13, 45, 58, 59: photo ©2013 Kids Only, a division of Jakks Pacific, Inc., used with permission. All rights reserved.

Cabbage Patch, pages 14, 33: photo by Marisa Train, © 2013 Christopher Byrne; page 15: photo ©2013 Christopher Byrne.

Care Bears, pages 14, 41: photo by Marisa Train, © 2013 Christopher Byrne.

Careful, pages 186, 187: photo by Marisa Train, © 2013 Christopher Byrne.

Chatty Cathy, pages 21, 22: photo by Marisa Train, © 2013 Christopher Byrne. Chatty Cathy® is a registered trademark of Mattel, Inc.

Clackers, page 119: photo by Marisa Train, ©2013 Christopher Byrne.

Colorforms, pages 82, 83: photo by Marisa Train, © 2013 Christopher Byrne.

Cootie, pages 172, 173: photo by Marisa Train, © 2013 Christopher Byrne.

Crayola 64 Box, page 87: photo by Marisa Train, © 2013 Christopher Byrne; Crayola 48 Box, page 64, photo ©2013 Crayola. All rights reserved. Photo used with permission.

Crazy Clock, pages 176, 177: photo by Marisa Train, © 2013 Christopher Byrne.

Creepy Crawlers Thingmaker, pages 80, 81, 94, 95: photo by Marisa Train, © 2013 Christopher Byrne. Creepy Crawlers® is a registered trademark of Mattel, Inc.

Dungeons & Dragons, pages 168, 194, 195, © 2013 Hasbro, Inc., used with permission.

Doodle Art, pages 80, 100, 101: PlaSmart Inc./The Original DoodleArt®, photo ©2013 All rights reserved. Used with permission.

Easy-Bake Oven, page 93: ©2013, photo by Christopher Byrne. Easy-Bake Oven® is a registered trademark of Hasbro, Inc.

Etch A Sketch, page 88, 89: Etch A Sketch is a registered trademark of The Ohio Art Company. Photos ©2013 The Ohio Art Company. All rights reserved. Photos used with permission.

Fashion Plates, pages 104, 105: photo by Marisa Train, © 2013 Christopher Byrne.

Frisbee, pages 48, 49: photo by Marisa Train, © 2013 Christopher Byrne; page 49, FRISBEE® is a registered trademark of Wham-O. Photo ©2013 Wham-O. All rights reserved of Wham-O. Photo ©2013 Wham-O. All rights reserved.

G.I. Joe, page 138: photo by Marisa Train, © 2013 Christopher Byrne; pages 126, 136, 137, 138: © 2013 Hasbro, Inc. Used with permission. G.I. Joe is a registered trademark of Hasbro, Inc.

Give-A-Show Projector, page 228, 229: photo by Marisa Train, © 2013 Christopher Byrne. Give-A-Show Projector® is a registered trademark of Hasbro, Inc.

Green Ghost, pages 168, 179: photo by Marisa Train, © 2013 Christopher Byrne.

Gumby, pages 219, 220: photo by Marisa Train, © 2013 Christopher Byrne.

Hands Down, pages 188, 189: photo by Marisa Train, © 2013 Christopher Byrne.

He-Man, pages 156, 157, 158, 177: photo by Marisa Train, © 2013 Christopher Byrne. He-Man® is a registered trademark of Mattel, Inc.

Hot Wheels, pages 146, 147: photo by Marisa Train, © 2013 Christopher Byrne. Hot Wheels ® is a registered trademark of Mattel, Inc.

Hula Hoop, page 110: photo ©2013 Maui Toys, a division of Jakks Pacific, Inc. Used with permission. All rights reserved; pages 108, 110, 112, 113 HULA HOOP® toy hoop is a registered trademark of WHAM-O. Photos ©2013 Wham-O. All rights reserved. Photo used with permission.

Hungry Hungry Hippos, pages 198, 199: photo by Marisa Train, © 2013 Christopher Byrne. Hungry Hungry Hippos® is a registered trademark of Hasbro, Inc.

Johnny Seven O.M.A., pages 140, 141: © 2013 Christopher Byrne.

Johnny Reb Cannon, pages 132, 133: photo by Marisa Train, © 2013 Christopher Byrne.

Ker-Plunk, pages 19, 66, 70, 71: © Mattel, Inc. All rights reserved.

King Zor, page 70: photo © 2013 Paul Reinhol. All rights reserved. Used with permission; page 70–71, courtesy of the author.

LEGO, pages 204, 205, 206: LEGO is a trademark and/or copyright of The LEGO Group. Photos © 2013 The LEGO Group. All rights reserved. Photos used with permission; page 207, photo used with permission from Barry Schwartz.

Lite-Brite, pages 80, 98, 99: © 2013 Hasbro, Inc. Used with permission. Lite-Brite® is a registered trademark of Hasbro, Inc.

Liddle Kiddles, pages 24, 25: photo by Marisa Train, © 2013 Christopher Byrne; Liddle Kiddles® is a registered trademark of Mattel, Inc.

Little People, pages 212, 213: photo by Marisa Train, © 2013 Christopher Byrne; Little People® is a registered trademark of Mattel, Inc.

Magic 8 Ball, pages 202, 211: © 2013 Mattel, Inc. All rights reserved.

Major Matt Mason, page 142: photo by Marisa Train, © 2013 Christopher Byrne; page 143, 145, courtesy of the author. Major Matt Mason® is a registered trademark of Mattel, Inc.

Matchbox, pages 130, 131: photo by Marisa Train, © 2013 Christopher Byrne. Matchbox® is a registered trademark of Mattel, Inc.

MicroMachines, pages 162, 163: photo by Marisa Train, © 2013 Christopher Byrne. Micro Machines® is a registered trademark of Hasbro, Inc.

Mouse Trap, pages 168, 174, 175: photo by Marisa Train, © 2013 Christopher